WHY TOLERATE RELIGION?

WHY TOLERATE RELIGION?

Brian Leiter

PRINCETON UNIVERSITY PRESS

Princeton and Oxford

Copyright © 2013 by Princeton University Press

Published by Princeton University Press,
41 William Street, Princeton, New Jersey 08540

In the United Kingdom: Princeton University Press,
6 Oxford Street, Woodstock, Oxfordshire OX20 1TW

press.princeton.edu

Library of Congress Cataloging-in-Publication Data

Leiter, Brian.
Why tolerate religion? / Brian Leiter.
p. cm.
Includes bibliographical references (p. xxx) and index.
ISBN 978-0-691-15361-2 (hardcover : alk. paper)
1. Religious tolerance. 2. Freedom of religion. I. Title.
BL640.L45 2013
323.44′2—dc23
2012010977

British Library Cataloging-in-Publication Data is available

This book has been composed in Garamond Premier Pro
Printed on acid-free paper. ∞

Printed in the United States of America

3 5 7 9 10 8 6 4

For Samuel
who had to endure a "day in hell"
with the intolerant

CONTENTS

CONTENTS

PREFACE AND ACKNOWLEDGMENTS

My interest in the topic of religious toleration arose when teaching at the University of Texas–Austin and witnessing in the years 2001 to 2008 the pernicious influence of reactionary Christians on both politics and public education in the state. Although some of their conduct might well fall beyond the protection of the principle of toleration defended in this book, reflection on religion and toleration led me to conclusions friendlier to religious belief than I would have imagined before undertaking systematic work on the topic.

Because I am centrally interested in the question of whether there is a moral reason to single out matters of religious conscience for special legal consideration and solicitude, I made the decision to consider moral arguments deriving from the two major, modern traditions of moral thought—the Kantian or deontological, and the utilitarian—without taking a side with either. This will, I hope, give the conclusion of the argument a broader resonance than would a partisan account of the moral foundations of religious liberty. As a representative of the deontological tradition, I have focused on John Rawls's account in his 1971 book *A Theory of Justice*, eschewing the later, and to my mind unfortunate, development of Rawls's views in *Political Liberalism*. The account in *A Theory of Justice* has the virtue of grounding liberty of conscience in considerations with immediate intuitive resonance and it also avoids the later Rawls's conflation of questions of political psychology and sociology (e.g., how can a liberal political and social order be made legitimate in the eyes of its subjects?) with questions about the correct or most plausible justification of fundamental political institutions.[1] For the utilitarian tradition, I draw on John Stuart Mill, and some more recent utilitarian-derived treatments of liberty of conscience. I also assume, as will become clear, that religious belief always involves some degree of *false* or at least *unwarranted* belief, but unlike some recent writers, it seems to me this fact about religious belief does nothing to settle the question of the scope of toleration. So, too, we can acknowledge that religion has often been the source of war, civil strife, and persecution, and yet recognize that it has also been the source of courageous resistance to injustice and movements for social and moral progress. Neither the putatively "bad" effects of religion nor the putatively "good" effects of religion will easily settle the question of the moral justification for distinctively *religious* liberty. Nor will they settle the question, taken up in chapter 5, of when and whether the establishment or disestablishment of religion is incompatible with principled toleration.

Because I am interested in making the argument accessible to scholars outside philosophy, I have largely avoided going into the minutiae of internecine debates among academic philosophers in the various camps. (I have also tried to keep the text free of technical debates among legal scholars.) I have occasionally noted some complications presented by such debates in the notes, but the aim has been to make the text readable by scholars in other disciplines interested in these issues, and perhaps also by educated laypeople.

The text incorporates—though with significant revisions to the account of religion—material from two earlier articles I have written on this subject: "Why Tolerate Religion?" *Constitutional Commentary* 25 (2008): 1–27, and "Foundations of Religious Liberty: Toleration or

Respect?" *San Diego Law Review* 47 (2010): 935–59. I am grateful to those journals for permission to incorporate some of that material in this book.

The material in these essays and in other parts of the book has benefitted from presentations on many occasions, including: the 'Or 'Emet Lecture at Osgoode Hall School of Law, York University, Toronto; the Leon Green '15 Lecture in Jurisprudence at the University of Texas School of Law; a keynote address at the Graduate Conference sponsored by the Department of Philosophy at Virginia Polytechnic Institute and State University; a public lecture sponsored by the Department of Philosophy at Colgate University; the Kline Colloquium sponsored by the Department of Philosophy at the University of Missouri–Columbia; the conference "Respect, Global Justice, and Human Rights" at the University of Pavia, Italy; the Law and Philosophy Workshop at the University of Michigan, Ann Arbor; the MacMillan Center Initiative on Religion, Politics, and Society at Yale University; a session of the Society for Applied Philosophy at the Eastern Division meeting of the American Philosophical Association in New York; the Analytic Legal Philosophy conference at New York University; the conference "Freedom of Conscience" sponsored by the Institute for Law and Philosophy at the University of San Diego; the Second Annual Law and Religion Roundtable at Northwestern University School of Law; the Legal Theory Workshop at Columbia Law School; and faculty workshops at the University of Chicago Law School (on three occasions), Cornell Law School, Chicago-Kent College of Law, University of Minnesota Law School, Fordham Law School, the Dickinson School of Law at Pennsylvania State University, and Queen's University Faculty of Law in Kingston, Ontario.

For their helpful comments on some or all of this material, I am grateful to Larry Alexander, Robert Audi, Mitch Berman, Akeel Bilgrami, Anu Bradford, Curtis Bridgeman, David Brink, Emanuela Ceva, Jane Cohen, Stanley Corbett, John Deigh, Rosalind Dixon, Michael Dorf, Christopher Eisgruber, David Enoch, Strefan Fauble, Victor Ferreres, Chad Flanders, Ranier Forst, William Fox, John Gardner, Tom Ginsburg, Naomi Gouldner, Leslie Green, Kent Greenawalt, Abner Greene, Ross Harrison, Scott Hershovitz, Kenneth Himma, Robert Hockett, Tony Honoré, Mark Hopwood, Paul Horwitz, William Hubbard, Shelly Kagan, Avery Katz, David Kaye, Brian Kierland, Andrew Koppelman, Ben Laurence, Ethan Lieb, Adrienne Martin, Richard McAdams, Adam Muchmore, Martha Nussbaum, Michael

Stokes Paulsen, Richard Posner, David Rabban, Peter Railton, Samuel Rickless, Larry Sager, Adam Samaha, Micah Schwartzman, Scott Shapiro, Steven Shiffrin, Sheila Sokolowski, Jim Staihar, David Strauss, Cass Sunstein, Nelson Tebbe, Matt Teichman, Patrick Todd, Kevin Toh, Mark van Roojen, Gerhard Wagner, Jeremy Waldron, and Michael White.

The penultimate version of the manuscript benefitted from very helpful written comments from an anonymous referee for Princeton University Press; from Richard Kraut, who kindly taught the material in his seminar at Northwestern University; and from the participants in the conference on the manuscript organized by Damiano Canale and Giovanni Tuzet at Bocconi University in Milan in October 2011: Giorgio Pino, Mario De Caro, Dimitrious Kryitsis, Emanuela Ceva, José Louis Martí, and Lorenzo Zucca.

I am grateful to John Wasserman, University of Chicago Law School class of 2012, for high-quality research assistance over the last two years. Alex Langlinais, a PhD student in philosophy here at the University of Chicago, provided invaluable assistance in readying the manuscript for publication. Rob Tempio at Princeton University Press has my gratitude for his long-standing interest in the project and his support throughout.

Thanks, as always, to Sheila, Samuel, William, and Celia for love, friendship, charm, smarts, good cheer, and inspiration. Grandpa Maurice is probably less friendly to religion than I am, but he still deserves credit (or blame!) for some aspects of the general outlook. The book is dedicated to Samuel, who survived the intolerant and then wrote about it with style and insight.

WHY TOLERATE RELIGION?

Introduction

A boy, age fourteen, enters his new middle school classroom on the first day of the year, wearing, as usual, his dagger. The teacher, alarmed, alerts the principal, who phones the police: carrying weapons is, of course, forbidden in school, and the police promptly confiscate the boy's dagger.

A straightforward case, perhaps, but not if the boy in question is a devout Sikh. For in the Sikh religion, male believers must wear a *kirpan*, a dagger or sword, as a symbol of their religious devotion. In many jurisdictions, in both North America and Europe, Sikhs have had to challenge laws that prohibit the carrying of weapons in school, since these laws would block discharge of their religious obligations. And on many occasions, Sikhs have been granted exemptions from those laws, on the grounds that freedom of religion requires the state to tolerate an exception to the general prohibition. The conscientious obligation a devout Sikh has to wear a kirpan is thought to be too serious—too important for the integrity and identity of this religious believer—to require him to forgo it because of the general prohibition on what anyone else would see as a weapon and danger to school safety.

But now suppose that our fourteen-year-old boy is not a Sikh but a boy from a rural family whose life "on the land" goes back many generations. As in almost all cultures, this boy's community has rituals marking the arrival of maturity for males in that community. A central one is the passing of a dagger or knife from father to son, across the generations. To be a "man" at the age of thirteen or fourteen is to receive that dagger from one's father, just as he received it from his, and so on, stretching back for decades, perhaps centuries. A boy's identity as a man in his community turns on his always carrying the family knife, for it marks his maturity and his bond with the past. There can be no doubt in this case about the conscientious obligation every boy of knife-bearing age feels to carry his knife with him, even in school. And there can be no doubt that were his ability to carry his knife abridged, his identity as a man devoted to his community would be destroyed.

There is no Western democracy, at present, in which the boy in our second scenario has prevailed or would prevail in a challenge to a general prohibition on the carrying of weapons in the school. Were he a Sikh he would stand a good chance of winning. But if he can only appeal to a century-old tradition, central to his identity, to which he feels categorically bound by his family traditions and upbringing, he is out of luck. The central puzzle in this book is why the state should have to tolerate exemptions from generally applicable laws when they conflict with *religious* obligations but not with any other equally serious obligations of conscience.

I start out by assuming that the moral ideal of toleration—of "putting up with" practices of which one disapproves because it is morally right to do so—provides the best justification for our Western ideal of religious liberty. I develop some familiar (at least to moral and political philosophers) arguments for that ideal. I then ask whether there is any reason to think that moral ideal would only single out religious claims of conscience, protecting our Sikh boy but leaving our rural boy with no legal remedy. This requires an account of what makes religious claims of conscience distinctive, the subject of chapter 2. I then show in chapter 3 that the best arguments for the moral ideal of toleration would not favor singling out only religion, as understood in chapter 2, for special exemptions from generally applicable laws.

Chapter 4 considers the possibility that the analysis has gotten off on the wrong foot: perhaps the moral ideal underlying religious liberty is not one of toleration but some more demanding concept of *respect* for religion. I consider various possible ways of understanding that more demanding ideal, and conclude that there is no reason to think religious claims of conscience would warrant them.

Finally, chapter 5 confronts the question of what to do about our Sikh boy and our rural boy if there really is no reason to tolerate only the former's claim of conscience for carrying a weapon in places where that is ordinarily prohibited. I argue that both boys should be out of luck: that there should not be exemptions to general laws with neutral purposes, unless those exemptions do not shift burdens or risks onto others. I also consider whether the moral ideal of toleration, as I articulate and defend it in this book, is incompatible with state establishment or disestablishment of religion generally. I argue that it is not, and that a tolerant state could, in principle, be either a religious or antireligious one.

CHAPTER I

Toleration

Religious toleration has long been the paradigm of the liberal ideal of toleration of group differences, as reflected in both the constitutions of the major Western democracies and in the theoretical literature explaining and justifying these practices. The American Constitution provides that "Congress shall make no law respecting an establishment of religion, or prohibiting the free exercise thereof."[1] As the German Constitution (or "Basic Law") provides in Article 4, "Freedom of faith and of conscience, and freedom to profess a religious or philosophical creed, shall be inviolable," adding, in a separate clause, "The undisturbed practice of religion shall be guaranteed."[2] The first of the four "Fundamental Freedoms" in the Canadian Charter of Rights and Freedoms is held to be "freedom of conscience and religion."[3] And Article 18 of the Universal Declaration of Human Rights declares,

> Everyone has the right to freedom of thought, conscience and religion; this right includes freedom to change his religion or belief, and freedom, either alone or in community with others and in public or private, to manifest his religion or belief in teaching, practice, worship and observance.[4]

While the American Constitution only mentions religion,[5] the recognition for claims of "conscience" in the other documents is more perfunctory than substantive: litigated cases overwhelmingly involve claims of religious conscience.[6] Indeed, if claims of religious conscience were not really the primary concern in each case, then surely the explicit mention of religion (or the mention of special protections for religion) would appear redundant on the protection purportedly afforded claims of conscience more generally.

While the historical reasons for the special "pride of

place" accorded religious toleration are familiar,[7] what may be more surprising is that no one has been able to articulate a credible *principled* argument for tolerating religion *qua* religion—that is, an argument that would explain why, as a matter of moral principle, we ought to accord special legal and moral treatment to religious practices. There are, to be sure, principled arguments for why the state ought to tolerate a plethora of private choices and conscientious commitments, as well as related practices of its citizenry, but none of these single out religion for anything like the special treatment it is accorded in existing Western legal systems. So why tolerate religion? The answer in this book is: not because of anything that has to do with it being religion as such—or so I shall argue.

Principled Toleration

To see why this is so we will need to start, though, with some distinctions that make possible a more perspicuous formulation of the question. In particular, we need to state clearly what is at stake in something called a *principle of toleration*. I shall take as a point of departure a useful formulation of the issues by the late English philosopher Bernard Williams:

> A practice of toleration means only that one group as a matter of fact puts up with the existence of the other, differing, group. . . . One possible basis of such an attitude . . . is a virtue of toleration, which emphasizes the moral good involved in putting up with beliefs one finds offensive. . . . If there is to be a question of toleration, it is necessary that there should be some belief or practice or way of life that one group thinks (however fanatically or unreasonably) wrong, mistaken, or undesirable.[8]

For there to be a *practice* of toleration, one group must deem another differing group's beliefs or practices "wrong, mistaken, or undesirable" and yet "put up" with them nonetheless. That means that toleration is not at issue in cases where one group is simply *indifferent* to another. I do not "tolerate" my neighbors who are nonwhite or gay because I am indifferent as to the race or sexual orientation of those in my community. Toleration, as an ideal, can only matter when one group *actively* concerns itself with what the other is doing, believing, or "being." Obviously, in many cases, the attitude of indifference is actually morally preferable to that of toleration: better that people should be indifferent as to their neighbors' sexual orientation than that they should disapprove of it but tolerate it nonetheless.

But a *practice* of toleration is one thing, a *principled reason* for toleration another. Many practices of toleration are not grounded in the view that there are *moral* reasons to tolerate differing points of view and practices, that permitting such views and practices to flourish is *itself* a kind of good or moral right, notwithstanding our disapproval. Much that has the appearance of principled toleration is nothing more than pragmatic or, we might say, "Hobbesian" compromise: one group would gladly stamp out the others' beliefs and practices, but has reconciled itself to the practical reality that it can't get away with it—at least not without the intolerable cost of the proverbial "war of all against all." To an outsider, this may look like toleration—one group seems to put up with the other—but it does not embody what Williams called a "virtue" of tolerance (or what I will call "principled tolerance"), since the reasons for putting up are purely instrumental and egoistic, according no weight to moral considerations. One group puts up with the other only because it would not be in that group's interest to incur the costs required to eradicate the other group's beliefs and practices.

Yet it is not only Hobbesians who mimic commitment to a principle of toleration. On one reading of John Locke,[9] his central nonsectarian argument for religious toleration is that the coercive mechanisms of the state are ill-suited to effect a real change in *belief* about religious or other matters. Genuine beliefs, sincerely held, can't be inculcated at gunpoint, as it were, since they respond to evidence and norms of rational justification, not threats.[10] In consequence, says the Lockean, we had better get used to toleration *in practice*—not because there is some principled or moral reason to permit the heretics to flourish but because the state lacks the right tools to cure them of their heresy, to inculcate in them the so-called correct beliefs.

Locke, it is fair to say, did not fully appreciate the extent to which states and—in capitalist societies—private entities can employ sophisticated means to effectively coerce belief, means that are both more subtle and more effective than he imagined. That history offers up so many examples of societies in which the tyranny of the few over the many is accepted by the many as a quite desirable state of affairs is compelling evidence that states can successfully inculcate beliefs, even dangerously false beliefs. Locke's "instrumental" argument for a practice of toleration should provide little comfort to the defender of toleration given his (understandable) failure to appreciate the full complexity of the psychology and sociology of belief inculcation.

Not only Hobbesians and Lockeans, however, mimic principled toleration. A variation on the Lockean instrumental argument for toleration is apparent in a popular theme in American political thinking—one that receives a well-known articulation in Frederick Schauer's defense of free speech[11]—according to which government *cannot be trusted* to discharge the task of intolerance "correctly"—that is, in the right instances. Speech can harm, in all kinds of ways, notes Schauer, and the various rationales for putting up with these harms—from John Stuart Mill's "marketplace of ideas" to Alexander Meiklejohn's conception of free speech as essential to democratic self-government—almost all fall prey to objections of one kind or another. But, says Schauer, there is still a reason to demand that the state tolerate many different kinds of speech (even harmful speech), and that is because *there is no reason to think the state will make the right choices* about which speech ought to be regulated. Schauer calls this "the argument from governmental incompetence" and writes,

> Freedom of speech is based in large part on a distrust of the ability of government to make the necessary distinctions, a distrust of governmental determinations of truth and falsity, an appreciation of the fallibility of political leaders, and a somewhat deeper distrust of governmental power in a more general sense.[12]

It is not, then, as in the Lockean argument, that government lacks the right means for bringing about intolerant ends; it is rather that government is not *competent*—that is, cannot be relied upon—to deploy its means in the right cases. Perhaps this kind of *instrumental* argument for state toleration is more plausible, but its justificatory structure makes it no different from that of the Lockean's: it does not tell us why we, morally, ought not to eradicate differing beliefs or practices, it tells us only that we (through the instrumentality of the state) are unlikely to do it right.

Where a genuine "principle of toleration" gets its purchase is in the cases where one group (call it the "dominant" group) actively disapproves of what another group (call it the "disfavored" group) believes or does; where that dominant group has the means at its disposal to *effectively* and *reliably* change or end the disfavored group's beliefs or practices; and yet still the dominant group acknowledges that there are *moral* or *epistemic* reasons (that is, reasons pertaining to knowledge or truth) to permit the disfavored group to keep on believing and doing what it does. That is "pure" or "principled" toleration,[13] and the question, then, is whether there is such a reason to tolerate religion.

My concern here shall mainly be with the principled grounds of *state* toleration, as opposed to toleration in interpersonal relations, though the issues are often similar. Some contemporary "liberal" philosophers think the right posture for the modern state is one of neutrality, not toleration, with the disapproval the latter implies. But I reject the view that any state can really be neutral in this way; as I will argue in chapter 5, every state stands for and enacts what I call a "Vision of the Good"—even if most Western democratic states no longer endorse such a distinctively religious vision. The American state has decided not only that "liberty and equality for all"

are fundamental values but that all children must learn
Charles Darwin's theory of evolution by natural selection, yet they do not need to "know" anything about the
biblical view of creation. The American state is not at
all neutral with respect to those sects that reject "liberty
and equality for all," let alone those that think creation
myths are on a par with biology and deserve equal time
in the public schools. Toleration thus remains a virtue for
the liberal state, as it does for the individual. Even if one
thinks states can aspire to more neutrality than I suppose,
it is still the case that when particular minority claims of
conscience, religious or otherwise, assert the need to be
exempted from neutral laws of general applicability, what
they are demanding is not neutrality but something like
the virtue of toleration—that is, they are demanding that
the state suspend its pursuit of the general welfare in order
to tolerate (i.e., "put up with") a conscientious practice
of a minority of its citizens that is incompatible with it.
That is why the central question in this book is: what are
the principled reasons why the state should exempt religious claims of conscience from the burden of its laws? I
frame the problem in these terms because, even though
the historical problem about religious toleration was
generated by conflict among religious groups, the contemporary problem, at least in the post-Enlightenment,
secular nations (of which the United States may still be

one) is different: it is why the state should tolerate religion *as such* at all.

Arguments for Principled Toleration

Before we consider religious tolerance in particular, it will be useful to consider the general structure of principled arguments for state toleration of group differences. The literature on the subject is voluminous, so necessarily I will be able to consider only a few themes here. Yet the themes I emphasize will, I believe, capture the main principled positions in the debates.

We can distinguish between two broad classes of principled arguments for toleration, which I will call *moral* and *epistemic* (though the latter ultimately rests on moral considerations as well). The strictly *moral* arguments for toleration claim either that there is a *right* to the liberty to hold the beliefs and engage in the practices of which toleration is required; or that toleration of those beliefs and practices is essential to the realization of morally important goods. The moral arguments divide, predictably enough, into Kantian and utilitarian forms.[14]

As paradigmatic of the broadly Kantian arguments, consider the Rawlsian theory of justice according to which "toleration . . . follows from the principle of equal liberty,"[15] one of the two fundamental principles of justice that, Rawls argues, rational persons would choose in what he calls the "original position"—that is, a situation in which people choose the basic principles of justice to govern their societies, and in which they do so deprived of the kind of information about their place in society that would render their judgments partial and self-serving. As Rawls puts it,

[T]he parties must choose principles that secure the integrity of their religious and moral freedom. They do not know, of course, what their religious or moral convictions are, or what is the particular content of their moral or religious obligations as they interpret them.... Further, the parties do not know how their religious or moral view fares in their society, whether, for example, it is in the majority or the minority.... [E]qual liberty of conscience is the only principle that the persons in the original position can acknowledge. They cannot take chances with their liberty by permitting the dominant religious or moral doctrine to persecute or to suppress others if it wishes. Even granting ... that it is more probable than not that one will turn out to belong to the majority (if a majority exists), to gamble in this way would show that one did not take one's religious or moral convictions seriously, or highly value the liberty to examine one's beliefs.[16]

Notice that nothing in this argument is specific to religion: the argument, as Rawls says quite clearly, is on behalf of rights securing "liberty of conscience," which can include, of course, matters of conscience that are distinctively religious in character but are not limited to them.[17] The argument depends only on the thought that persons in the "original position" know that they will have certain convictions about how they *must* act in certain circumstances—convictions rooted in reasons central to the integrity of their lives.

The utilitarian arguments have a similar feature—namely, that they do not obviously single out religion for special consideration as opposed to other important matters of conscience. These arguments come in many different varieties, but all share, in one form or the other, the core idea that it maximizes human well-being—however exactly that is to be understood—to protect liberty of conscience against infringement by the state.[18]

Why does it promote human well-being to protect liberty of conscience? Many arguments trade, at bottom, on a simple idea: namely, that *being able to choose what to believe and how to live* (within certain side-constraints, about which more shortly) makes for a better life. Being told *what you must believe* and *how you must live*, conversely, make lives worse. I shall gloss this simple thought as the "private space argument." It maximizes human well-being, so the argument goes, if, within certain limits, individuals have a "private space" in which they can freely choose what to believe and how to live.

Is it true that granting individuals a private space maximizes human well-being? Could it be that many, perhaps even most, individuals make themselves miserable—that is, worse off—precisely because they make foolish choices about what to believe and how to live?— Or perhaps because they don't make *real* choices at all, being hostage to social and economic milieux and enjoying only the *illusion* of choice? These illiberal thoughts—familiar to readers of Plato, Karl Marx, and Herbert Marcuse, among many others—have little purchase these days within the mainstream of English-speaking moral and political theory, though not, as far as I can tell, because they have been refuted systematically.[19] For the sake of argument here, I shall put these doubts to one side and grant that the private space argument is plausible, and thus states a utilitarian ground for toleration. Notice, too, that it states a more capacious ground for liberty of choice than the Rawlsian argument, which seems delimited to matters of conscience (matters, for example, about which there are very weighty reasons, central to personal integrity and so on).

In contrast to the moral arguments for toleration that we have just considered, *epistemic* arguments for toleration emphasize the contribution that tolerance makes to *knowledge.* Such arguments find their most systematic articulation in the work of John Stuart Mill. According to Mill,[20] toleration is necessary because (1) discovering the truth (or believing what is true *in the right kind of way*) contributes to overall utility; and (2) we can only discover the truth (or believe what is true *in the right way*) in circumstances in which different beliefs and practices are permitted to flourish. The first premise in the Millian argument for toleration is, quite obviously, a moral one: we should care about the truth (or believing the truth in the right kind of way) because of the contribution that makes to the morally valuable end of utility. Friedrich Nietzsche, among others, denies the moral premise: the "truth is terrible," he says,[21] by which he means precisely that sometimes knowing the truth is incompatible with life, a fortiori, with utility (though utility was not, of course, Nietzsche's particular concern).

It is only the second premise of the Millian argument

for toleration that is distinctively epistemic, for it is this premise that claims that toleration of divergent beliefs and practices contributes to knowledge of the truth. Note that the "truth" at issue for Mill concerns both truths about "facts" as well as truths about "value"—in particular, moral truths about the best kinds of lives available to creatures like us. From an epistemic point of view, both factual and moral truths have several features in common. First, in neither case are we justified in assuming that we are infallible: we may be wrong, and that is a reason to permit dissident opinions, which may well be true. Second, even to the extent our beliefs are partially true, we are more likely to appreciate the whole truth to the extent we are exposed to different beliefs that, themselves, may capture other parts of the truth. Third, and finally, even to the extent our present beliefs are *wholly* true, we are more likely to hold them for the right kinds of reasons, and thus more reliably, to the extent we must confront other opinions, even those that are false. For all these epistemic reasons, toleration of a wide array of expression of differing beliefs is warranted according to Mill.

Moral truths, however—that is, truths about how we *ought* to live—supply the ground for a wider scope of toleration, one that encompasses *practices*, not just *beliefs*.

For the epistemic conditions for the discovery of moral truths require not only that we be exposed to differing beliefs, but that, as Mill puts it, "the worth of different modes of life should be proved practically" through what he calls "experiments in living."[22] In other words, to know how we really ought to live, it is not enough to hear differing opinions expressed on the subject; one must have the empirical evidence provided by lives actually lived in accordance with different guiding principles. It is only, for example, by seeing (or, better yet, experiencing) the lives of a pig satisfied and Socrates dissatisfied (in Mill's famous example) that we can come to the knowledge that the latter life is better—that is, involves higher-quality pleasures—than the former.

Before we turn to the special case of religious toleration, we need to call attention to one more feature of principled arguments for toleration: namely, that they all recognize *side-constraints* on the scope of toleration.[23] Even if there is a right to liberty of conscience that demands state tolerance of differing beliefs and practices, as Rawls holds; or even if toleration promotes overall utility or happiness—or facilitates a kind of knowledge that promotes overall utility—as the utilitarian arguments hold; it is still the case that there are *limits* on how much toleration the state must display toward acts of conscience.

For the Rawlsian, "The limitation of liberty is justified only when it is necessary for liberty itself, to prevent an invasion of freedom that would be still worse," so "liberty of conscience is to be limited only when there is a reasonable expectation that not doing so will damage the public order which government should maintain." "This expectation," Rawls also says, "must be based on evidence and ways of reasoning acceptable to all. . . ."[24] For the utilitarian, by contrast, the side-constraints on toleration are typically set by some version of Mill's famous Harm Principle, according to which "the only purpose for which power can be rightfully exercised over any member of a civilized community, against his will, is to prevent harm to others."[25]

On either theoretical approach, the limits of tolerance are set by the liberty interests or well-being of others in the community, and these limits have their primary impact not on toleration of *beliefs* but on toleration of the *practices* or *actions* undertaken in accord with those beliefs. The state will still, on either the Rawlsian or Millian view, it seems, have to tolerate some religious group's belief that adherents of all other religions are heretics, destined for damnation; but the state need not tolerate that same group's desire to act on its beliefs by, for example, killing the infant children of the alleged heretics before their souls are corrupted, and thus eternally damned, by heresy.

Cases like these are, of course, the easy cases on any view of toleration and its limits. Much harder are two other kinds of cases: first, those involving the expression of beliefs that have as their probable (but not certain) consequence actions that infringe upon liberty or are otherwise likely to cause prohibited harms; and second, those involving practices or actions that have as their probable (but not certain) consequence the infringement of liberty or the causing of prohibited harms.

Mill is, of course, thinking of the first category of cases when he writes,

[E]ven opinions lose their immunity when the circumstances in which they are expressed are such as to constitute their expression a positive instigation to some mischievous [i.e., harmful] act. An opinion that corn dealers are starvers of the poor, or that private property is robbery, ought to be unmolested when simply circulated through the press, but may justly incur punishment when delivered orally to an excited mob assembled before the house of a corn dealer.[26]

That same thought is codified in American constitutional law by the doctrine that speech that poses what used to be called a "clear and present danger" can be suppressed by the state.[27] This approach supposes that you can hold and express any belief *unless* there is a "tight" causal nexus between expression of the belief and forbidden acts. The Rawlsian view seems to come to the same thing, though the metaphors Rawls employs are different: the threat to liberty, he says, for example, "must be securely established by common experience."[28] The Rawlsian formulation does not as obviously incorporate a requirement that the resultant harm be as *immediate* or *imminent* as do the Millian examples or the American constitutional doctrine. It suffices on the Rawlsian view that the causal nexus between expression of belief and liberty-infringing act be "securely established." To be sure, the criteria for *securely* establishing that nexus may only be satisfied in the same cases of *immediate* or *imminent* harmful conduct contemplated on the Millian view, which is reason to think they come to the same thing.[29]

The second category of cases presents the same issue: that is, there are practices based on beliefs that it seems *ought* to be tolerated (on either the Millian or Rawlsian view), about which we can ask whether those practices might stand in a causal nexus with harm that satisfies the applicable evidential standards. A 2006 Canadian case, *Multani v. Commission scolaire Marguerite-Bourgeoys*,[30] involving the right of Sikhs to carry the *kirpan* (a ceremonial knife), as required by their religion—even in schools—illustrates this issue. Those opposing the practice argued, in part, that this religious practice poses too great a risk of harm, reflected on the general ban of weapons in school; the other side argued, by contrast, that the probability of harm was very slight, as evidenced, for example, by the fact that there was no known instance of a kirpan being used as a weapon. The Canadian Supreme Court, of course, opted for toleration of the practice of carrying the kirpan, given the importance of the practice to the believers, the putatively slight risk of harm, and the special value multiculturalism is assigned in the Canadian Charter. (We shall return to this case in chapter 3.)

CHAPTER II

Religion

In asking whether there is something *special* about religion that bears on religious toleration, we are not asking whether there is some feature (or features) of religious belief and practice that warrant principled toleration of religion on either *moral* or *epistemic* grounds. There plainly are such features, for example, that religious beliefs are often matters of *conscience*, and thus would fall within the scope of any argument, like the Rawlsian one, for protecting liberty of conscience. If there is a special reason to tolerate religion it has to be because there are features of religion that warrant toleration, and these features are either

1. features that *all and only* religious beliefs have, either as a matter of (conceptual or other) necessity
   or as a contingent matter of fact; or

2. features that other beliefs have, or might have, but
   which in these other cases possession of the features
   would not warrant principled toleration.[1]

I am hard-pressed to think of features of religion that
satisfy the second category, so I shall put that possibility to one side here. Are there, then, features of religious
belief that, either necessarily *or* simply contingently, distinguish religious beliefs from other kinds of belief that
might warrant toleration?

Beyond Law and Durkheim

The general question of what distinguishes "religion" has
been extensively discussed in the constitutional literature in the United States, though typically with an eye
to purely doctrinal questions about the meaning of a particular constitutional provision within a particular constitutional tradition and sociopolitical context.[2] Being

concerned with questions of statutory or constitutional meaning, these approaches do not necessarily grapple with what makes religion *morally* or *epistemically* distinctive from the standpoint of principled toleration, and some even try to dodge the inquiry altogether.[3] The inquiry here is to figure out *what is distinctive about religion* such that religion *ought* to be tolerated, quite apart from any particular legal regime. An answer to that question will permit us then to return to actual constitutional protections to see whether they are justifiable from a principled point of view (the subject of chapter 5).

Something similar may be said of the most common social-scientific approaches to religion, many of which rely, explicitly or implicitly, on Émile Durkheim's famous account of religion.[4] For Durkheim, religion consists of "beliefs and rites," where the rites are distinguished "by the special nature of their object" and that object is fixed by the religious beliefs—thus, for Durkheim, "only after having defined the belief can we define the rite."[5] Durkheim astutely observes that "belief" in "divine" beings would be inadequate to characterize religion, since it would appear to rule out Buddhism and Jainism as religions right at the start.[6] Instead, Durkheim proposes that a religion is a "unified system of beliefs and practices relative to sacred things, that is to say, things set apart and forbidden—beliefs and practices which unite into one single moral community called a Church, all those who adhere to them."[7] This attempt to identify the phenomenon of religion no doubt has significant virtues for social-scientific purposes,[8] but somewhat less so for ours (though I will follow Durkheim in treating *belief* as having explanatory primacy, though not quite for his reasons).

The most immediate difficulty is that the notion of the "sacred"—"things set apart and forbidden," whose opposite is the "profane"[9]—is now doing the key analytical work. (The social and communal dimension is clearly of secondary importance in Durkheim's theory—it is introduced only to distinguish "magic" from "religion"[10]—and would, on its own, do little to distinguish ethnic, cultural, even sports-based communities.) Yet even if we suppose that this characterization was adequate to pick out religious beliefs and practices, it would leave mysterious why such beliefs and practices should command special moral and legal consideration. As the various constitutional provisions quoted at the start of chapter 1 made clear, and as the moral arguments developed in that chapter confirm, if there is something morally important about religious belief and practice that demands legal solicitude, it is connected to the demands of conscience that religion imposes upon believers. Those demands may sometimes map onto what Durkheim calls the "apart and forbidden," but what gives them special moral standing is their etiology in conscience, not that they demand "standing apart" and "respecting the forbidden."

A final, but important, methodological note before we turn to the substance of my proposed analysis. Any examination of religion ought to do some justice to our pretheoretical intuitions about what counts as religion. An analysis according to which Catholicism is not a religion, but devotion to one's favorite football team in the World Cup is a religion, is prima facie (and probably irredeemably) deficient. But pretheoretical intuitions about what counts as religion are not the only relevant considerations. Most important, we want to identify religion in such a way that we can see why it has some moral and possibly legal claim on special treatment. To that end, if the best analysis of religion—one that identifies what makes it distinctive *and* suggests why it has a claim on toleration—requires us to forfeit some of our pretheoretical intuitions, that may be the cost of clear thinking about religious toleration and its parameters. We shall return to these considerations later.

Defining Religion

The legal philosopher Timothy Macklem is somewhat unusual in having addressed our central question directly in his 2000 article "Faith as a Secular Value" and in his recent book on the philosophical foundations of the individual liberties.[11] According to Macklem, what distinguishes religious belief is that it is based on *faith*, not *reasons*. As he puts it,

> faith itself provides the moral basis for freedom of religion. . . . At its most basic level, the concept of faith describes the manner in which a particular belief or set of beliefs may be subscribed to by human beings. In that sense of the word, faith exists as a form of rival to reason. When we say that we believe in something as a matter of faith . . . we express a commitment to that which cannot be established by reason, or to that which can be established by reason but not for that reason.[12]

According to Macklem, faith is required "where the quest for reasons is impossible, but commitment [even without reasons] is potentially valuable" and so, even from a secular perspective, we have reason to value faith and tolerate it.[13]

Remarks by a prolific American scholar of law and religion, John Witte Jr., suggest a second important feature of religion for purposes of our question. Witte broaches familiar themes when he writes,

[R]eligion is special and is accorded special protection in the [American] Constitution. . . . The founders' vision was that religion is more than simply a peculiar form of speech and assembly, privacy and autonomy. Religion is a unique source of individual and personal identity, involving "duties that we owe to our Creator, and the manner of discharging them," as Madison put it. Religion is also a unique form of public and social identity, involving a vast plurality of sanctuaries, schools, charities, missions, and other forms and forums of faith.[14]

Although these themes are familiar, most of them seem to me to be clearly false, at least in the world today. Religion is not "a unique source of individual and personal identity"; the hundreds of millions of people who have no religious beliefs presumably still have individual and personal identities, defined by sundry other systems of belief—moral, cultural, ethnic, professional, and so on. It also seems dubious that religion is "a unique form of public and social identity" as purportedly evidenced by the institutions that operate in the name of religion. Politics, class, ethnicity, cultural traditions, and so on all seem to play the same kind of role, in some instances, much more powerfully than religion does (think of France or England). Where Witte is onto something important, I think, is in calling attention to the religious idea of "duties that we owe to our Creator, and the manner of discharging them." Many religious commands have a kind of *normativity*, a kind of motivational force for persons—perhaps, *but not necessarily*, in virtue of their being "owed to [a] Creator"—that may indeed distinguish them in important ways.

Following the leads of Macklem and Witte, I suggest that two features single out "religious" states of mind from others. The first pertains to the normativity of (at least some) religious commands; the second pertains to the relationship between (at least some) religious belief and evidence. On my proposed account, for all religions, there are at least some beliefs central to the religion that

1. issue in *categorical* demands on action—that is, demands that must be satisfied no matter what an individual's antecedent desires and no matter what incentives or disincentives the world offers up;[15] and

2. do not answer ultimately (or at the limit) to *evidence* and *reasons*, as these are understood in other domains concerned with knowledge of the world. Religious beliefs, in virtue of being based on "faith," are insulated from ordinary standards of evidence and rational justification, the ones we employ in both common sense and in science.[16]

I shall refer to this first feature as the *categoricity of religious commands* and the second as religious belief's *insulation from evidence*. Categoricity, it is important to emphasize, will be treated primarily as a property of how the religious commands are *experienced by believers*, though often enough the experience will track the formulation of religious or theological doctrine. But what makes categoricity of religious commands such a significant feature of religion—indeed, of all claims of conscience, not only religious claims[17]—is the way it manifests itself in the behavior of believers. Insulation from evidence, by contrast, will be understood usually as a claim about the religious doctrine rather than about the typical epistemic attitudes of believers. Obviously, fanatics will hold any set of beliefs *regardless of the evidence*, and we often characterize fanatical adherence to a doctrine, pejoratively, as a kind of "religious" devotion to it. But a fanatical defender of the theory of gravity, for example, who does not even worry about how evidence of the expansion of the universe squares with his theory, would hardly show that we ought to characterize the theory of gravity as a religious doctrine, insulated from reasons and evidence. There may be some hard cases at the margins (we will return to those below), but in general, we should ask whether the beliefs in question, correctly understood, are supposed to be insulated from reasons and evidence, not whether some believers so hold them.[18]

Notice that *beliefs* or the attitudes of *believers* are central to the analysis of religion precisely because it would be hard to see how mindless, habitual, or merely casual religious *practices* could claim whatever moral solicitude is due matters of *conscience*.[19] It is precisely because of the underlying beliefs that we think the actions required by them deserve special moral and perhaps legal consideration. No one, after all, thinks mindless or habitual behavior *per se* has a claim on special legal or moral consideration (and, by the same token, such behavior is unlikely to come into conflict with the law, since those whose religious practices are merely habitual or casual are far more likely to alter them when confronted with legal sanction than are those who view them as matters of conscience).

Needless to say, the categoricity of religious commands accounts for both one of the most admirable and one of the most frightening aspects of religious commitment—namely, the willingness of religiously motivated believers to act in accordance with religious precepts, notwithstanding the costs. (This, of course, is why serious religious believers are responsible for most of the major litigation about the law of religious liberty in the United States and elsewhere.[20]) Thus we find the devoutly religious among those who were at the forefront of domestic resistance to Nazi oppression in the 1930s,[21] and the injustice of apartheid in South Africa from the 1960s onward and in America in the 1950s and '60s.[22] We also, of course, find the devoutly religious among those who bomb abortion clinics and fly airplanes into buildings. These religiously inspired individuals risk (and often suffer) death, injury, and prison in order to comply with their religious conscience. It is painfully familiar, of course, that in all these cases adherents of the very same religion contested whether the actions of these believers were sanctioned, let alone commanded, by the religious doctrine. (Religious leaders, to take but one example, were also at the forefront of defense of apartheid in the United States in the 1950s and '60s.) The important fact here, however, is that religious commands—whether rightly or wrongly understood—are taken categorically by their adherents.

Refining the Definition: Problems of Under- and Overinclusion

Is religion really alone in this regard? One respect in which Marxism may have been justifiably called a religion is precisely that in some of the historical contexts just noted, the only other groups as categorically committed to resistance as the religiously inspired were communists, who led resistance to Nazism, as well as apartheid in both South Africa and the United States, long before other groups joined the battle. More generally, of course, one might think that *all commands of morality* are categorical in just this way. Does that mean, then, that religion is not special after all, since it shares the property of categoricity of its commands with Marxism and with one common understanding of morality?

We can easily distinguish the case of moral commands.[23] To be sure, there are theoretical understandings of morality—Immanuel Kant's most famously, though not only his—according to which the demands of morality are indeed categorical. What is interesting and important about religion is that it is one of the few systems of belief that gives effect to this categoricity. Pure Kantian moral agents are few and far between (I think I can count them on one hand, and probably have fingers left over!), but those who genuinely conduct their lives in accord with the categoricity of the moral demands they recognize are overwhelmingly religious.

But not all of them are, of course, and this is where the case of Marxists and other similar "believers" become relevant. Here, though, we need to attend to the second purportedly distinctive feature of religious belief—namely, its insulation from evidence and reasons. Whatever the historical and philosophical verdict on the evidence and reasons supporting Marxism, one very clear difference is that Marxism took itself to be answering to—not insulated from—standards of evidence and reasons in the sciences, in a way that religion has not.[24] Marx, as is well-known, conceived of his theory as a "scientific" account of historical change, and thus it had to answer to the same standards of evidence and justification as any other scientific theory. (That is why it has been possible to refute historical materialism by counterexample.[25]) Nothing similar, of course, is true of any of the major religious traditions: all countenance at least some central beliefs that are not ultimately answerable to evidence and reasons as these are understood elsewhere (e.g., in common sense and in science). This is why Macklem was correct to emphasize that the distinctively religious state of mind is that of *faith*—that is, believing something *notwithstanding the evidence and reasons* that fail to support it or even contradict it.

Even here, of course, we need to be careful. There are, for example, "intellectualist" traditions in religious thought—William Paley's "natural theology" or neo-Thomist arguments come to mind[26]—according to which religious beliefs (for example, belief in a creator or, as in America recently, belief in "an intelligent designer") are, in fact, supported by the kinds of evidence adduced in the sciences, once that evidence is rightly interpreted. It is doubtful, though, whether these intellectualist traditions capture the character of popular religious belief, the typical epistemic attitudes of religious believers. (To the extent the same is true of "popular" Marxist belief—that is, the epistemic attitudes of committed communists—that may well be good reason to describe Marxism as a kind of religion in those cases.) But even putting popular religious belief to one side, there remain important senses in which intellectualist traditions in religious thought might still be thought of as *insulated from evidence*. First, of course, it is dubious (to the put matter gently) that these positions are really serious about following the evidence where it leads, as opposed to manipulating it to fit preordained ends. Second, and relatedly, in the case of the sciences, beliefs based on evidence are also revisable in light of the evidence; but in the intellectualist traditions in religious thought just noted, it never turns out that the fundamental beliefs are revised in light of new evidence.[27] The whole exercise is one of post-hoc rationalization, as is no doubt obvious to those outside the sectarian tradition. Religious beliefs are *purportedly* supported by evidence, but they are still insulated from revision *in light of evidence*.[28]

But is there not a more banal sense in which many religious believers, especially in certain Christian sects, claim to find evidential support for the reasonableness of their beliefs?[29] Might not a Catholic, for example, quite reasonably appeal to testimonial evidence, as recorded in the Bible and elsewhere, in support of her belief in the resurrection of Jesus Christ? Certainly that is compatible with there still being *some* beliefs part of the Catholic religion that are insulated from reasons and evidence, but it does suggest how a religious believer might, in fact, claim that some rather central beliefs of her religion are, in fact, responsive to reasons and evidence without subscribing to a more ambitious "intellectualist" interpretation.

Certainly testimonial evidence is a kind of evidence that plays a role in ordinary life and sometimes in scientific inquiry, but in both common sense and science it plays a role quite different than it does in the kind of purported evidence-based justification for belief in the resurrection of Christ. Ancient testimonial evidence in favor of events that are inconsistent with all other scientific knowledge about how the world works is nowhere thought to constitute good evidence for belief in a particular proposition, and that is exactly the status of the putative evidence in support of the resurrection of Christ. To say that some core beliefs in any religion are insulated from reason and evidence as understood in the sciences is to make a claim not only about the *kinds of evidence* but about the *kinds of epistemic weight* such evidence has in deciding what to believe. To be sure, testimony that Christ rose from the dead is a kind of colorable evidence from a scientific point of view; that the testimony is inconsistent with everything we have reason (evidence) to believe about what happens when human bodies expire—both from massive amounts of testimonial evidence, as well as the evidence of physiology and biology—indicates that the ancient testimonial evidence deserves no credence at all. In that respect, devout Catholics who still persist in believing in the resurrection of Christ hold that belief insulated from reasons and evidence.

The two features of religious belief under consideration so far—*categoricity* and *insulation from reasons and evidence*—suggest another possible case of under-inclusiveness in the account of religion, one that would conflict sharply with our pretheoretical intuitions about what counts as a religion. For it is not at all obvious that Buddhism is characterized by categoricity and insulation from reasons and evidence. The matter is complex because, as one scholar has observed, Buddhism is more a "nebula rather than a unified religion,"[30] comprising diverse schools and culturally specific traditions. A certain Western perception of Buddhism became dominant in the nineteenth century when "triumphant rationalism was seeking an alternative to Christianity" and so Buddhism was reinterpreted from being "a religion revealed by a transcendent God" to being "a human, moral, and rational religion founded by an extremely wise individual."[31] This view of Buddhism is evident even in someone like Friedrich Nietzsche, who was no rationalist.[32] Nietzsche favorably contrasts Buddhism with Christianity on the grounds that it "is a hundred times more realistic than Christianity" by "posing problems objectively and coolly":

> Buddhism is the only genuinely positivist religion in history. . . . [I]t no longer says "struggle against *sin*" but, duly respectful of reality, "struggle against *suffering*." Buddhism is profoundly distinguished from Christianity by the fact that the self-deception of the moral concepts lies far behind it. . . .
>
> The *two* psychological facts on which it is based and which it keeps I mind are: *first*, an excessive sensitivity, which manifests itself in a refined susceptibility to pain; and *second*, an overspritualization . . . which has damaged the instinct of personality by subordinating it to the "impersonal." . . . These physiological conditions have led to a depression, and the Buddha proceeds against this with hygienic measures . . . [such as] life in the open air, the wandering life; moderation in eating . . . ; wariness of

all intoxicants; wariness also of all emotions that activate the gall bladder or heat the blood; no *worry* either for oneself or for others. . . .

Prayer is ruled out, and so is *asceticism;* there is no categorical imperative, no *compulsion* whatever, not even in the monastic societies (one may leave again).[33]

Nietzsche's Buddhism is just the instrumental rationality of a person afflicted by hypersensitivity to pain and discomfort, and its only imperatives are *hypothetical*, not categorical: *if* you want to relieve your suffering, then embrace the "Four Noble Truths" of the Buddha and follow "the Eightfold Path" to salvation. Rather than being insulated from reasons and evidence, Buddhism so conceived—as "a genuinely positivistic religion" (as Nietzsche puts it)—says, *Here is the cause of your suffering, and here is the cure, in light of the actual facts about human suffering.*

On this interpretation, Buddhism might seem to stand apart from the world's other major religions, but this rationalist gloss on Buddhism does not do justice to the complexities of doctrine and practice. Most obviously, every religion could be reinterpreted as a bit of instrumental rationality of the form: *if you want to be saved/redeemed, do X.* Every believer of every religion has already made that instrumental choice (or had it made for him by parents or others), such that rejecting the end (salvation or, in the Buddhist case, "enlightenment") is now off the table as a meaningful option; that is why at least some of the commands of the religion are now experienced as *categorical.* Moreover, and contrary to the rationalist picture of Buddhism, "[r]itual is even omnipresent within sects that claim to be antiritualistic, such as Zen," as one scholar notes, adding that ritual here means not only "prayer, reciting the scripture, icon worship" but also "the smallest actions in everyday life (meals, works, etc.)."[34] Whether such Buddhist rituals have a *categorical* character is a harder question, but at least some aspects of typical Buddhist doctrine, even across sects, seem to: for example, the requirement not to harm any living creature,[35] a requirement embedded in a general metaphysical picture of time, reincarnation, and karma that quite clearly is insulated from the standards of reasons and evidence operative in common sense and the sciences.[36] Notwithstanding Buddhism's denial of a god/creator, it is surely these other features that are a significant part of the explanation for the pretheoretical intuition that Buddhism, too, is one of the world's major religions.

Now consider a different kind of case—pertaining not to the *underinclusiveness* of the characterization but its *overinclusiveness*—that might raise doubts about whether *categoricity of commands* and *insulation from evidence* are sufficient to distinguish religious belief and practice. Think, for example, of the Maoist personality cult that gripped China during the Cultural Revolution in the 1960s.[37] Here masses of individuals acted on commands from Chairman Mao Zedong that they took to be, in effect, categorical, and that they carried out without regard to evidence, including evidence of the substantial harms inflicted on individuals and, ultimately, society as a whole (though arguably evidence of these latter harms was less apparent at the time). Does this make the Maoist personality cult a religion? Perhaps we should so describe it, yet this seems to run roughshod over distinctions it seems worth drawing. Pretheoretically, after all, we might think totalitarian personality cults are distinct from religions, even if in some historical and cultural contexts their nature and effects are the same. But what marks the difference, given that it is not the *categorical* character of their commands or the *insulation* of their core beliefs from evidence? One plausible idea is that religious beliefs not only involve categorical commands and insulation from evidence, but also:

3. religious beliefs involve, explicitly or implicitly, a *metaphysics of ultimate reality*.

But what is it to endorse a "metaphysics of ultimate reality"? Such a metaphysics seems to be distinguished, in part, by the relationship in which it stands to the *empirical evidence of the sciences*: namely, that such a view about the "essence" or "ultimate nature" of things neither *claims support from empirical evidence* nor *purports to be constrained by empirical evidence* (its claims "transcend" the empirical evidence, hence its "metaphysical" character). In this regard, though, (3) seems to be only a variation on the idea that religious belief is *insulated* from evidence—insulated not only in the sense that it does not answer to empirical evidence but also in the sense that it does not even *aspire* to answer to such evidence.

The latter point may capture the *metaphysical* character of the beliefs, but it is still silent on the sense in which they concern *ultimate reality*. *Ultimate* in this context has less to do, I think, with metaphysical gradations of what is *essential* (whatever that would mean) than it does with questions of *value:* the ultimate reality is the aspect of reality that is most important for valuable/worthwhile/desirable human lives, whether that concerns the transcendent well-being of the "soul," or the moral value of life in this, the material world. The *categoricity of commands* distinctive of religious beliefs are, in turn, related to this *metaphysics of ultimate reality* in the sense that they specify what *must* be done in order for believers to stand in the right kinds of relations to "ultimate reality"—that is, to the reality that makes their lives worthwhile and meaningful.[38]

Will the addition of a third distinctive characteristic of religious belief rule out personality cults of the Maoist variety? There is some reason to think so. First, the Maoist-style personality cults may ordinarily be *de facto* insulated from evidence, but they are less often *de jure* insulated: that is, they *purport* to answer to facts and evidence in a way that metaphysical claims about ultimate reality do not even purport to do so.[39] Second, the personality cults, focused as they are on the personality of the leader, have an only indirect connection to the nature of ultimate reality, one contingent on the extent to which the leader is interested in those kinds of questions. To the extent a personality cult is de jure insulated from evidence and the "dear leader's" commands are directly related to his view of ultimate reality, then to that extent we may need to revise the pretheoretical intuition (if we share it) that personality cults are different from religious beliefs.

Although a *metaphysics of ultimate reality* may be a third essential feature that distinguishes religious belief from the beliefs held by participants in personality cults, for purposes of the question of whether there is a principled reason for toleration of *religion qua religion*, only the first two features, I will argue, matter. This is because the second feature, *insulation from evidence* (especially de jure insulation from evidence), already captures what is significant—namely, the *metaphysical* character of religious beliefs about ultimate reality. By contrast, so many different systems of belief involve views about ultimate reality—and such views almost all qualify for toleration under the rubric of *conscience* (subject, of course, to the usual side-constraints)—that the fact that religious beliefs also involve such views won't generate any special reason for toleration that does not attach in virtue of the first two distinctive features of religious belief.

This leaves us, then, with a final possible (and perhaps the most worrisome) case of overinclusiveness in the proposed account of religion—namely, morality itself. For is not morality characterized both by categoricity of its commands and its insulation from reasons and evidence (as reasons and evidence are understood in the sciences)? Now as noted earlier, categoricity is not necessarily a feature of morality, though it is, to be sure, central on many theoretical understandings; and religion, as we also observed earlier, may make categoricity motivationally effective in a way that it would not otherwise be. But what of insulation from reasons and evidence? Is moral belief necessarily insulated from reasons and evidence? What we say about morality on this score depends, ultimately, on what we take to be the relevant metaphysics and semantics of morality—that is, on whether we take moral facts to exist and how we interpret the meaning of judgments about what is morally right and wrong. So, for example, for cognitivist realists like Richard Boyd and Peter Railton[40]—philosophers who think that moral judgments express beliefs about the moral character of the world, beliefs that are sometimes true—moral judgments are not insulated from reasons and evidence as they are understood in the sciences; indeed, just the opposite.[41] So on this view, morality is not at all like religion; it answers to reasons and evidence—and answers successfully! Noncognitivist antirealists, by contrast, conceive of moral judgments not as expressing beliefs (which might be true or false) but as expressing mental states that are not truth-apt, such as feelings. On this picture, then, moral judgments are by their nature insulated from reasons and evidence; just as feeling cheerful or sad is not answerable to reasons or evidence, so too with moral judgment.[42] Religious judgments are still different, on this account, since some religious judgments *do express beliefs* and so, in principle, could be answerable to reasons and evidence, but are nonetheless taken to be insulated from them. So on either of the two main contenders for a credible metaphysics and semantics of morality, morality is still different from religion.

That is a somewhat technical philosophical explanation for why moralities are not religions on my account, but perhaps there is an even simpler route to blocking the assimilation of all morality to religion—namely, by adding a different, fourth condition to the basic account in terms of *categoricity of commands* and *insulation from evidence*—one that, unlike a *metaphysics of ultimate reality*, is not otiose given the first two. This new condition would take its cues from Arthur Schopenhauer's seminal account of religion, which is astutely summarized by Julian Young as follows:

[A] religion is something with four central and interconnected features: it provides a "solution" to the problem of death, a solution to the problem of pain, an exposition and sanctioning of the morality of the community of believers, and, finally, it is pervaded by a sense of mystery.[43]

Standing on its own, parts of this account would be obviously inadequate as an account of religion. There are, for example, many ways of dealing with death, pain, and suffering, ranging from philosophy to behavioral and cognitive therapy to pharmacology. But we might think that the other elements in Schopenhauer's account might be captured by *categoricity of commands* (that sounds a bit like sanctioning the morality of the community of believers) and *insulation from evidence* (that sounds a bit like mystery). So what distinguishes religion, then, would be the categoricity of its commands and its insulation from evidence, but also that there are some beliefs in the religion that

4. render intelligible and tolerable the basic existential facts about human life, such as suffering and death.

I will refer to this final characteristic of religion as *existential consolation*. The addition of existential consolation to our account of religion has the virtue of clearly excluding the case of Maoist personality cults, of Marxism, and (probably) of morality (though perhaps some moral systems, like the Kantian, might be construed as also discharging the task of a kind of existential consolation as well—but certainly the conclusion that Kantian ethics has a religious character is not so counter-intuitive as to be dismissed out of hand). It also captures a feature of religious belief and practice that explains its central importance in so many human lives.

If, then, the *categoricity of its commands, insulation from evidence* (not just de facto, but also de jure) and *existential consolation* are the distinctive features of religious belief—not, to be clear, the features that necessarily make religious beliefs important and meaningful to people but the features that distinguish religious beliefs from other equally important and meaningful beliefs—do the principled reasons for tolerance reviewed earlier warrant singling religion out for protection? It is to this question that we now turn.

CHAPTER III
Why Tolerate Religion?

In chapter 1, we considered three categories of principled arguments for toleration: two kinds of moral arguments, one deontological (illustrated by John Rawls), and one utilitarian; and an epistemic argument, exemplified by John Stuart Mill, though one ultimately based on utilitarian considerations as well. If I am right about the features that distinguish religious belief, is there any reason to think that principled toleration demands tolerance of those beliefs *in particular*?

I think we may safely bracket the Rawlsian moral argument for toleration, since it is hard to see how persons in Rawls's original position, operating behind the "veil of ignorance," could reason, in particular, about the value of insulation from evidence and the categoricity of demands, let alone existential consolation. To be sure, Rawls allows that those in the original position do know that they will recognize categorical demands, though they do not, of course, know what those will be. Rawls writes, "An individual recognizing religious and moral obligations regards them as binding absolutely in the sense that he cannot qualify his fulfillment of them for the sake of greater means for promoting his other interests."[1] But this grounds, in Rawls's view, the argument for the general principle of equal liberty of conscience—individuals in the original position "cannot take chances with their liberty,"[2] as he says—not anything specific to religion. Indeed, Rawls repeatedly lumps religious and moral categoricity together, so that it is fair to say that the only thing individuals behind the veil of ignorance know is that they will accept some categorical demands, not they will accept distinctively religious ones—that is, ones whose grounding is a matter of faith.[3] If that is right, then the Rawlsian perspective cannot help us evaluate the principled case for toleration of religion *qua* religion.

It may also seem that we can dispense with the *epistemic* arguments for toleration equally quickly. There is no reason to think, after all, that tolerating the expression of beliefs that are *insulated from evidence and reasons*—that is, insulated from *epistemically relevant* considerations—will promote knowledge of the truth. Bear in mind, though, that Mill is not concerned only with *knowing* the truth but believing what is true for the right kinds of reasons. Perhaps exposure to opinions that are insulated from reasons and evidence is, itself, a spur to better reasons for believing what we ought to believe? That is certainly possible, but it is hard to see why it is likely to be the case.

Yet this dismissal of the epistemic argument would be far too quick.[4] For only if we already suppose that the only epistemically relevant considerations are those having to do with evidence and reasons as understood in both common sense and the sciences would we be entitled to conclude that beliefs insulated from these kinds of considerations do not contribute to knowledge of the truth. Indeed, it might seem to be precisely in the spirit of Millian epistemic libertarianism to think that alternative epistemic methods (or methods that *purport* to have epistemic payoffs) be permitted in the interests of discovering new truths.

We must be cautious here, however, about the proper extension of the Millian view. For even Mill, recall, believes that there is no epistemic reason for the "free market" of ideas and arguments in the case of mathematics (geometry in particular): "there is nothing at all to be said on the wrong side of the question [in the case of geometry]. The peculiarity of the evidence of mathematical truths is that all the argument is on one side."[5] This is all the more striking in light of the fact that Mill is a radical empiricist, and so denies that there is any a priori knowledge: even logical and mathematical truths are a posteriori, vindicated by inductive generalizations based on past experience. On the Millian view, then, there simply is no epistemic case for making room for, as an example, "mathematics based on faith," on the grounds that new truths might be uncovered.

Might we not generalize the point? Because religious belief is insulated from the standards of evidence and reasons that have been vindicated a posteriori since the scientific revolution, one might think that, as with mathematics, there is a Millian reason to think that any wholesale departure from these epistemic standards is tantamount to a wholesale abandonment of epistemically relevant considerations, as my original formulation of the "quick" response proposed.[6] Religious belief, on this account, really is marked by its insulation from the *only* epistemically relevant considerations, the latter point (so it is claimed) vindicated a posteriori as in the case of mathematics. The claim about a posteriori vindication of certain epistemic standards is, itself, a controversial one, and much will ultimately turn on the details of what we take the historical record to show.[7] So perhaps there is a weaker but still pertinent response to the challenge to what is supposed to count as epistemically relevant considerations for purposes of the Millian epistemic argument for toleration. For even if we allow that there is an epistemic reason to tolerate purportedly epistemically relevant considerations different than those that figure in common sense and the sciences, there will now be nothing in this argument that singles out religious "faith" for special solicitude, since it is only one of a multiplicity of nonstandard methods that purportedly provide access to truths (consider telepathy, talking with the dead, clairvoyance, etc.). Even if there is a viable epistemic argument for toleration of beliefs insulated from the familiar standards of evidence and reasons, that argument does not help single out religious belief for special protection.

Of course, on the Millian view, there is a second kind of epistemic goal at issue—namely, knowing how one *ought* to live; a kind of knowledge requiring "experiments in [different kinds of] living." Perhaps, then, a different epistemic argument for tolerance of religious beliefs in particular is that living in accord with categorical demands that are unhinged from reasons and evidence is one of the "experiments" we ought to encourage through a regime of toleration?[8]

Toleration, however, operates under side-constraints, as we discussed in chapter 1. Being a genocidal white supremacist, after all, is an "experiment in living," but the Millian (or even the Rawlsian) argument from toleration does not suppose that we ought to tolerate that experiment given the harm it can be reasonably expected to cause. And that brings us to the crux of the issue as to whether there is a *special* reason to tolerate religion qua religion. *If* what distinguishes religious beliefs from other important and meaningful beliefs held by individuals is that religious beliefs are *both* insulated from evidence *and* issue in categorical demands on action, then isn't there reason to worry that religious beliefs, as against other matters of conscience, are *far more likely* to cause harms and infringe on liberty?[9] And might that not even form the basis of an argument for why there are special reasons *not* to tolerate religion?

Now, such a demeaning conclusion about religious belief would certainly be congenial to many nonbelievers,[10] but I wonder whether it is warranted. It is true that the combination of *categorical demands on action* and *insulation from evidence* seems a frightening one, but as we noted in chapter 2, it has often been responsible for laudatory and courageous behavior, such as resistance to Nazism and to apartheid. In capitalist societies, where market norms increasingly permeate all activities and values, one of the few sturdy bulwarks, with broad cultural resonance, against self-enrichment as the only "rational" end remains certain kinds of deep religious commitment. But even putting to one side the morally salutary effects of religious belief and practice, is there any reason to think that attention to evidence would preclude embrace of abhorrent categorical demands? Or, to put the point differently: why think the evidence would thwart grossly unjust categorical demands?

This raises vexed philosophical questions—for example, does knowledge of the facts require certain moral responses such that people sensitive to the evidence would not be capable of the atrocities so commonly perpetrated by religious zealots?—but we may bracket those here. For from the standpoint of a principled argument for toleration, the question is slightly different. The question is not whether toleration of *categorical demands on action* conjoined with *insulation from evidence* stands in the requisite causal nexus with harm or infringements of liberty such that we would be justified in *not* tolerating those kinds of beliefs. Rather, the question is whether there is any *special* reason to tolerate beliefs whose distinctive character is defined by the categoricity of its demands conjoined with its insulation from evidence. That is, we are still looking for a principled argument for tolerating religion qua religion; only if we found such an argument would we then have to address the question about the *limits* of that principle of toleration by reference to side-constraints. If it is true that beliefs that support categorical demands that are insulated from evidence have potential (perhaps even a *special* potential) for harms to well-being—and surely they do—then that would be reason to doubt whether any utilitarian argument for tolerating religion qua religion will succeed.

Could the fact that such beliefs also provide *existential consolation* save them from a utilitarian point of view? Let us suppose that existential consolation is a utility-maximizing achievement of religious beliefs, as it surely is on most conceptions of utility or well-being.[11] Would that then provide a utilitarian rationale for singling out matters of religious conscience for special protection, even conceding the potential (perhaps special potential) for harms to well-being that arise from the conjunction of categorical demands and insulation from evidence? The answer would only be affirmative if we were confident in the answer to two questions, one factual, one counterfactual. The factual question is, does the utility-enhancing function of religious beliefs (their ability to provide *existential consolation*) outweigh the potential for harm of the conjunction of *categorical demands* and *insulation from evidence*? The counterfactual question is, could the utility-maximizing effect of religious belief's *existential* consolation function be realized by beliefs (or other practices) that did not incorporate the potentially harmful attributes of categoricity and insulation from evidence? The answer to the latter question must surely be "yes." Throughout the world now, nonreligious individuals find ways of achieving existential consolation—from philosophical reflection, to meditation, to therapeutic treatment—that do not run any of the risks of commitment to belief systems involving the potentially harmful brew of categorical commands and insulation from evidence.

The answer to the first question is much harder to assess. As with most difficult issues demanding utilitarian calculation, we quickly enter the realm of rank speculation. The speculation required, however, must also now factor in to the calculus the affirmative answer to the counterfactual question. So the *existential consolation* function of religion only generates a utilitarian rationale for tolerating *religion qua religion* if we bite what I will call the "speculative bullet"—that is, only if we are willing to speculate that the existential consolation functions of religion produce more utility than the harm produced by the conjunction of categoricity and insulation form evidence; and only if we are willing to speculate that the preceding net gain in utility would be greater than the alternative ways of producing existential consolation without the conjunction of categoricity and insulation from evidence. It is not obvious, I dare say, why one would bite the speculative bullet, absent an antecedent bias in favor of religion.

Let us recap. There may be compelling principled reasons for the state to respect liberty of conscience—the conclusion established by the Rawlsian and Millian arguments of chapter 1—but there is no apparent moral reason why states should carve out special protections that encourage individuals to structure their lives around categorical demands that are insulated from the standards of evidence and reasoning we everywhere else expect to constitute constraints on judgment and action, even allowing that those demands may figure in systems of belief that have some utility-maximizing effects (e.g., existential consolation). Singling out religion for toleration is tantamount to thinking we ought to encourage precisely this conjunction of categorical fervor and its basis in epistemic indifference, and that we should simply bite the speculative bullet. If matters of religious conscience deserves toleration—as they surely do given the arguments of chapter 1—then they do so because they involve matters of *conscience*, not matters of religion.

We may conclude the discussion in this chapter by returning to a concrete case. Recall the Canadian Supreme Court case *Multani v. Commission scolaire Marguerite-Bourgeoys*,[12] affirming the right of a Sikh child to carry his ceremonial knife, the *kirpan*, in school, in accordance with his religion. Recall that those seeking to bar the carrying of the kirpan argued, in part, that this religious practice poses too great a risk of harm, which is why there is a general ban of weapons in school. Those defending the exception for the Sikh child argued, by contrast, that the risk of harm was very slight, and that a kirpan had never been used to attack anyone in a school previously. Although the Canadian Supreme Court allowed that the kirpan "undeniably has characteristics of a bladed weapon capable of wounding or killing a person" (¶37); that many Sikhs "wear a plastic or wooden kirpan" (¶37) which does not present these risks; and that carrying kirpans is, properly, prohibited in courts and on airplanes (¶62–64), the court nonetheless held that the student in question could carry the most dangerous kind of kirpan as long as "his personal and subjective belief in the religious significance of the kirpan is sincere" (¶37), including his "sincere" belief that wearing a plastic or wooden kirpan would not suffice—since adherents of a religion "may adhere to the dogma and practices of that religion to varying degrees of rigour" (¶39), apparently free from scrutiny by the state.

The extent to which the state must defer to the "dogma" of a "sincere" believer—whose beliefs issue in categorical commands unhinged from evidence (hence their dogmatic character)—is perhaps most apparent in the court's peculiar discussion of why the school setting is different from courtrooms and airplanes. Although there are obvious differences among these environments, the court laid most emphasis on its romantic view of schools as places where "both teachers and students are partners" rather than adversaries, such that it is "possible to better control the different types of situations that arise in schools" (¶65). Quite remarkably, no mention is made of the pertinent differences that might count in favor of stricter restrictions in schools, such as the absence of armed guards in many schools all of the time, and in all schools in at least some places some of the time; the literal immaturity and concomitant problems with impulse control characteristic of school populations; and the antagonistic relationships among students, and between teachers and students, that surely exist as often as the romantic "partnerships" the court envisions. Although the court opted for toleration of the *practice* of carrying the kirpan—given the importance of the practice to the believers, the putatively slight risk of harm, and the special value multiculturalism is assigned in the Canadian Charter—one might think the importance of side-constraints on toleration have particular force in cases like this. Certainly the state should tolerate the various religious practices of Sikhs under the general rubric of liberty of conscience, but it is hard to see why the same Harm Principle that countenances drawing the line at "ceremonial" knives on planes and in courtrooms should not apply as well in the classroom. Does any plausible conception of liberty of conscience demand that we accept one believer's view that *only real knives will do*, while other believers of the same faith are content with wooden ones? (Is there no existential consolation left over if the knife is wood rather than steel?) If the preceding argument is correct, it is not clear what moral argument could warrant that conclusion.

To what conclusions, then, are we entitled at this point? First, the argument suggests that there is no principled reason for legal or constitutional regimes to single out religion for protection; there is no moral or epistemic consideration that favors special legal solicitude toward beliefs that conjoin *categorical commands* with *insulation from evidence*, even if they produce some *existential consolation*. Second, the general principled arguments for toleration sketched in the preceding chapter—both the broadly Rawlsian and Millian ones—do justify legal protection for liberty of conscience, which would necessarily encompass toleration of religious beliefs. This means the *hard* question will be whether to expand the range of legal accommodations to *all claims* of conscience, an issue to which we will return in chapter 5. Third, and finally, the general reasons for being skeptical that there are special reasons to tolerate religion qua religion (because of the special potential for harm that attaches to the conjunction of categorical demands based on beliefs insulated from evidence) suggest that we must be especially alert to the *limits* of religious toleration imposed by the side-constraints.

CHAPTER IV

Why Respect Religion?

I have so far assumed that the moral foundation of the law of religious liberty is to be found in the idea of principled toleration. But am I entitled to that assumption? Martha Nussbaum, for example, has recently argued for the attitude of "respect" as the moral foundation of religious liberty,[1] though, as I will suggest, her account is ambiguous between two senses of respect.[2] In particular, I shall claim that in one sense of respect (hereafter, "minimal" respect), it is compatible with nothing more than toleration of religion; and that in a different sense (hereafter, "affirmative" respect, and which Nussbaum appears to want to invoke), it could not form the moral basis of a legal regime since religion is not the kind of belief system that could warrant that attitude.

What Kind of Respect?

"I really respect her intellect" and "You should show some respect for his feelings" both employ the same word, but express two different concepts of "respect": the former I will call the "affirmative" concept of respect, the latter the "minimal" concept. Nussbaum has defended an account of the moral foundations of the law of religious liberty as based on a principle of "equal respect for conscience,"[3] which she takes to be different from "mere" toleration of religion.[4] I shall argue that the minimal concept of respect does not, at least with regard to religion, move us far beyond the moral ideal of toleration, and that only if religion warrants the affirmative concept of respect would we have reason to think our law of religious liberty should answer to a more demanding moral standard.[5] In this chapter I argue that there is no case for application of the affirmative concept.

The minimal concept of respect—as expressed in "You should show some respect for his feelings"—maps onto what Stephen Darwall dubbed many years ago as "recognition respect."[6] This kind of respect, in Darwall's formulations, involves "giving appropriate consideration or recognition to some features of its object in deliberating about what to do," for example, "by being willing to constrain one's behavior in ways required by" those features.

In short, "Recognition respect for persons . . . is identical with recognition respect for the moral requirements that are placed on one by the existence of other persons."[7]

Darwall's recognition respect is a minimal form of respect in two regards: first, it is agnostic about any other dimension of value that might attach to the particular manifestations of the features of the object to which the respect is owed; second, it is silent on the nature of the "moral" constraints on behavior that are demanded by the respect. The first kind of minimalness is central to demarcating Darwall's recognition respect from its more affirmative cousin, what Darwall calls "appraisal respect" (about which more momentarily). The second kind of minimalness is what makes it hard to distinguish recognition respect from toleration, as I shall argue below.

If the claim "You should show some respect for his feelings" invokes the minimal concept of respect, the statement "I really respect her intellect" depends on a more affirmative concept, what Darwall dubs "appraisal respect." In Darwall's terminology, such respect "consists in an attitude of positive appraisal of that person either as a person or as engaged in some particular pursuit"; as a result it "is like esteem or a high regard for someone" and it is compatible with having no "particular conception of just what behavior *from oneself* would be required or made appropriate by that person's having the features meriting such respect."[8] When you "respect her intellect" you admire and appraise highly the caliber of her mind, whereas when you "respect his feelings" you act in such a way as to show an appropriate moral regard for how your actions might affect them.

Notice, again, that the minimal concept of respect—Darwall's "recognition respect"—makes no substantive *moral* demand on the kind of action that is appropriate: it requires only that one honor whatever "moral requirements . . . are placed on one by the existence of other persons." The substantive content of these moral requirements is open; indeed, it seems that recognition respect is morally otiose, "only an exhortation to perform the (other) duties that we already owe," as Leslie Green puts it.[9]

Yet appraisal respect also makes no substantive moral demand on action, but for a different reason: it demands only "esteem" or high appraisal of certain features of persons, not that one act toward them in a certain way. Yet appraisal respect can also result in moral demands on action, when the highly appraised features are ones with moral value or that one has a moral obligation to support or protect. One ought to "respect" genius, and the more genius there is in the world the greater the well-being of persons, or so one might think. So a certain kind of consequentialist might think that appraisal respect for someone's genius generates prima facie obligations toward that person.

Recognition respect demands only, to quote Darwall again, that one honor whatever "moral requirements . . . are placed on one by the existence of other persons." But surely among the "moral requirements" one has to abide by are those demanded by principled toleration, as I have already argued. Has one discharged all one's moral obligations of respect toward the religious beliefs and practices of a person if one tolerates them? Only an argument that morality demands more by way of our attitudes and practices toward religion would support a negative answer.

Nussbaum, in her recent lengthy defense of religious liberty (more precisely, liberty of conscience), thinks that tolerance of religion is "too grudging and weak" an attitude.[10] We need, she says, a "special respect for the faculty in human beings in which they search for life's ultimate meaning"—namely, their "faculty" of conscience.[11] We should follow Roger Williams in "rever[ing] . . . the sincere quest for meaning," since "everyone has inside something infinitely precious, something that demands respect from us all, and something in regard to which we are all basically equal."[12] But how can we distinguish "respect" here from toleration, the attitude Nussbaum deems "too grudging and weak"? We are all probably more or less equal in our capacity for self-deception, for example, but that demands nothing more than toleration: as long as your self-deception doesn't harm someone else, we ought to let it alone. So, too, it might seem with "conscience" and the "sincere quest for meaning": that ought to be tolerated, even when your "sincere quest for meaning" leads you to feel disgust for homosexuality as violating the dignity of the family.[13] Humans are roughly equal in many faculties, but it seems odd to think that deficient exercises of those faculties should elicit a moral attitude beyond that of tolerance.[14] That is the dilemma that afflicts something like Nussbaum's view of liberty of conscience[15]: yes, the faculty of conscience, which we all possess (however deficiently we exercise it), might be thought to elicit a kind of minimal recognition respect from others. But why is that minimal notion of respect not fully discharged by the moral attitude of toleration?[16]

Is Religion a Proper Object of Affirmative Respect?

So, can we justify *respect* for religious conscience in some sense stronger than the minimal kind of recognition respect discharged by toleration? I want to turn, again, to a contemporary philosopher who has grappled with a version of our issue—namely, Simon Blackburn.[17] Blackburn tells the story of being invited to dinner at a colleague's home and then being asked to participate in a religious observance prior to dinner. He declined, though his colleague said participating was merely a matter of showing "respect." His host seems to have viewed this as a matter of simple recognition respect, but Blackburn interpreted it (perhaps rightly) as something more:

I would not be expected to respect the beliefs of flat earthers or those of the people who believed that the Hale-Bopp comet was a recycling facility for dead Californians who killed themselves in order to join it. Had my host stood up and asked me to toast the Hale-Bopp hopefuls, or to break bread or some such in token of fellowship with them, I would have been just as embarrassed and indeed angry. I lament and regret the holding of such beliefs, and I deplore the features of humanity that make them so common. I wish people were different.[18]

Blackburn's reaction brings out starkly that recognition respect—which requires us to treat others as morality requires in virtue of some morally relevant attribute of theirs—does not entail that we view them as appraisal respect might require. Blackburn himself remarks that respect "is a tricky term" since it "seems to span a spectrum from simply not interfering, passing by on the other side, through admiration, right up to reverence and deference."[19] He dubs as "respect creep" the phenomenon by which "the request for thin toleration turns into a demand for more substantial respect, such as fellow-feeling, or esteem, and finally deference and reverence,"[20] which is what his dinner host expected and Blackburn declined to offer.

But given the ambiguity of "respect"—marked by the continuum from "toleration" to "esteem" and "reverence"—what is it that should incline one to one end of the spectrum or the other? Here Blackburn's own account of his resistance to offering the appraisal respect his host asked for is a bit unclear. We can distinguish three considerations:

1. *Religious belief is false belief.* The falsity of religious belief is clearly part of the reason Blackburn is resistant to offering it respect, but surely *falsity* is not enough. After all, if his host had asked that Blackburn raise his glass in a toast to "my beautiful and intelligent children," surely Blackburn would have raised his glass even if the

offspring were homely and dull-witted. We are, all of us, in the grips of a multitude of false beliefs—I believe you are enjoying this book, you believe your colleagues think well of you, she thinks her research breaks new ground, he believes he is a clever conversationalist—but these usually do not elicit disrespect, contempt, or ridicule from our peers. Indeed, one might well admire, for example, my confidence and a colleague's enthusiasm for her research, so the *falsity of belief* is plainly not enough to explain why there is a special problem about respect for religion.

2. *Religious belief is perniciously false belief.* This consideration, I suspect, comes closer to the mark for someone like Blackburn: it is not just that his host has false beliefs—though Blackburn's rhetoric could suggest that *is* the issue—but that he has false beliefs whose falsity is *pernicious.* False beliefs can be pernicious in various ways: for example, in how they affect the believer's behavior or to the extent they are part of an institutional web of false beliefs whose consequences are pernicious—licensing, for example, harassment of and discrimination against gay men and lesbians, attacks on science education in the schools, and opposition to valuable scientific research in a variety of areas. If Blackburn's host had said, "And now let us bow our heads in honor of my personal hero, Adolf

Hitler, a great and honest man who led the fight against the poisonous influence of world Jewry," one might easily understand Blackburn's refusal of recognition, let alone appraisal, respect: his host has a perniciously false belief. And if Blackburn were attending dinner with his host in North Carolina (one of his academic homes) in 1959, and the host had asked everyone to raise a glass "in salute to the brave leaders of the White Citizen's Council who strive to keep the Negro in the position to which his intellectual and moral character suits him," we can easily (at least today) understand why Blackburn would refuse, since the beliefs expressed are not only perniciously false but part of an institutional structure that caused immeasurable harm to human beings.

But these are not the dinners Blackburn attended. So our real question is whether there is any reason to think that a Jewish prayer before Friday evening dinner (what was at issue in Blackburn's case) is a case of comparably *pernicious* false belief in either sense? More generally, is there any reason to think religious belief *per se* is comparably pernicious?

3. *Religious belief is (epistemically) culpable false belief—* that is, it is unwarranted and one ought to know it is unwarranted. This is probably the real concern for

Blackburn, and it certainly distinguishes the case of religious belief from some of our other false beliefs, such as those involving our children or ourselves. (Blackburn's host may falsely believe his children are intelligent and attractive, but he is hardly epistemically blameworthy for so believing!) Why should *culpably false beliefs* elicit *respect* rather than indulgence or toleration? That is surely the point of Blackburn's scenarios such as being asked to "respect" those who believe the Hale-Bopp comet is a recycling facility for dead Californians. These beliefs are false, and ridiculously so, and no one in their right mind should accept them.

But are religious beliefs—say, belief in the resurrection of Jesus Christ, or in the existence of an omniscient, omnipotent, nonmaterial being—such beliefs? They differ from the Hale-Bopp beliefs in several obvious respects: they have more adherents, are more familiar to nonbelievers, and are more deeply integrated into the cultural and normative practices of our society, even among the normative practices of those who do not accept the beliefs in question. (Recall Friedrich Nietzsche's quip about putative "free thinkers" who say, "The church, *not* its poison [i.e., its moral teaching], repels us. . . . Leaving the church aside, we, too, love the poison."[21]) Is that enough to think they warrant respect in some sense more *affirmative* than mere toleration?

One might suppose, for all kinds of practical (e.g., Hobbesian) reasons, that the category of *widely accepted culpable false belief* deserves different treatment than the category of *idiosyncratic culpable false belief*, though it is hard to see why that would add up to anything like the affirmative kind of appraisal respect that Blackburn's host expected or Nussbaum's "precious faculty" account would suggest. So perhaps our focus should not be on the *quantity* of culpable false belief involved, but on its *culpability*, which seems to be the relevant factor. After all, if I believe that I am Zeus, and you are mere mortals and so should not be so insolent as to ask me hard questions about this book, then I have a culpably false belief, which does not warrant affirmative respect (and probably not even tolerance!).

Is our religious believer in the same situation? Certainly any answer depends, in the first instance, on the available evidence and thus the standards for what would constitute blameworthy epistemic irresponsibility.[22] In the fourteenth century, religious belief was quite plainly neither irrational nor unwarranted—and thus *not* culpably false belief—but after the Scientific Revolution and the Enlightenment, it is less clear. Of course, there is a large literature in Anglophone philosophy devoted to defending the rationality of religious belief.[23] I shall not, here, be able to address this literature in any detail. Suffice it to observe that its proponents are uniformly religious believers, and that much of it has the unpleasant appearance of post-hoc—sometimes desperately post-hoc—rationalization. Alex Byrne, a philosopher at the Massachusetts Institute of Technology, captures the dominant sentiment among other philosophers about this literature rather well:

> [I]t is fair to say that the arguments [for God's existence] have left the philosophical community underwhelmed. The classic contemporary work is J. L. Mackie's *The Miracle of Theism*, whose ironic title summarizes Mackie's conclusion: the persistence of belief in God is a kind of miracle because it is so unsupported by reasons and evidence.[24]

Of course, our prior account of what makes a matter of conscience *religious* did not include any reference to theism but to the *categoricity* of at least some religious commands, the fact that some religious beliefs are *insulated from evidence*, as evidence is understood in commons sense and the sciences, and the contribution of religious belief to *existential consolation*. (The insulation from evidence is, to be sure, central to what makes theism possible, as Mackie argues.) The so-called reformed epistemology of apologists for religious belief like William Alston and Alvin Plantinga is, thus, predicated on an attack on "Enlightenment-approved evidence."[25] I am going to assume—uncontroversially among most philosophers but controversially among reformed epistemologists—that "reformed epistemology" is nothing more than an effort to insulate religious faith from ordinary standards of reasons and evidence in common sense and the sciences, and thus religious belief is a *culpable* form of unwarranted belief given those ordinary epistemic standards. Even allowing that that is true, does it follow that such beliefs do not warrant a more affirmative kind of respect than mere recognition respect, which could be discharged by "toleration"?

To think there is a problem here, we do need to assume that *culpable failure of epistemic warrant* is a reason to withhold appraisal respect from a belief. Is that true? Often when we admire someone's *loyalty* or *devotion* to

a cause or a person, we admire their willingness to remain committed to it notwithstanding countervailing
evidence. She thinks her son is a wonderful pianist, even
though his piano teacher would sooner take gas than
give the boy another futile lesson. He continued to support Senator McCarthy's presidential bid in 1968, even
after it was clear one of the prowar candidates would get
the nomination. The mother and the supporter *ought*
to know better as a purely epistemic matter, but there is
something admirable about their stances. In these cases,
though, we think the *loyalty* or *devotion* has some value
either to the person or the cause so valued, or that it ex-
emplifies a trait of character or habit of mind that is otherwise valuable.

Let us suppose, as seems most plausible, that religious
belief in the post-Enlightenment era involves culpable
failures of epistemic warrant. Can it be redeemed by the
kinds of considerations just noted? This, it seems to me,
is the central and hard question about whether the law
of religious liberty should embody mere *toleration* or a
more affirmative kind of appraisal respect. Do matters
of conscience that issue in *categorical demands on action
and are insulated from reasons and evidence*, but which
also produce *existential consolation*, have a special kind of
value that we should appraise highly or *merely* tolerate?

It might be tempting in the United States in the early twenty-first century to think the answer obvious. After all—to take an example close to home—religious believers overwhelmingly supported George W. Bush, widely considered one of the worst presidents in the history of the United States, whom many think ought to be held morally culpable both for the illegal war of aggression against Iraq as well as the casualties resulting from domestic mismanagement. Of course, if we really thought there were some connection between religious belief and support for the likes of Bush, then even toleration would not be a reasonable moral attitude to adopt toward religion: after all, practices of toleration are, themselves, answerable to the Millian Harm Principle, and there would be no reason *ex ante* to think that Bush's human carnage is something one should tolerate.

But such a posture is not warranted: there is no reason to think that beliefs unhinged from reasons and evidence and that issue in categorical demands on action are especially likely to issue in "harm" to others. As I noted earlier, there are plenty of cases—for example, resistance to Nazism or opposition to apartheid—in which religious believers pursued what now seems the obviously morally correct course long before others. On the other side, take the au courant case of Bernard Madoff, who swindled thousands of individuals out of billions of dollars by promising unrealistic returns on purported "investments." Although Madoff exploited his religious connections, to be sure, it is quite clear that he himself was acting on the basis of hypothetical imperatives (where the consequent of each conditional was his own enrichment) that were keenly attuned to reasons and evidence: he was clearly an astute student of the facts about human psychology! Perhaps beliefs that issue in *categorical demands on action* and that are *unhinged from reasons and evidence* are more harmful, on average, but it seems to me much more empirical evidence would actually be required to support that conclusion.

Do we really need such evidence, though, to answer our initial question? The default position, as argued in chapter 3, is that we ought to *tolerate*—that is, show recognition respect—toward religious beliefs, but do we have any reason to accord them a more affirmative form of respect, such as Darwall's appraisal respect? That is the central issue here. And it is now difficult to see how any of the preceding considerations would support the conclusion that religious matters of conscience warrant esteem or reverence. Only if there were a *positive* correlation between beliefs that were *culpably without epistemic warrant* and valuable outcomes would it seem that we should think them proper objects of appraisal respect. But the evidence on this score is, as we have already had occasion to note, mixed.

Two Final Strategies for Establishing Religion as an Object of Appraisal Respect

Perhaps the argument for appraisal respect for religious beliefs and practices could be redeemed by the following argument.[26] Think of the National Science Foundation or the National Endowment for the Humanities. Most of the work these institutions fund turns out to be of little or no value to anyone other than the grant recipient. Some of it is positively dreadful or, in retrospect, foolish. Yet we might have reason to appraise these institutions highly because they do make possible some research of great value by anyone's estimation. Since we have conceded already that religious commitment, with its distinctive commitment to *categoricity* and *indifference to reasons and evidence*, is in fact conducive to distinctively good outcomes in certain circumstances (e.g., resistance to fascists and racists), and since we have also noted the positive contribution to *existential consolation* made by religious belief, might we not have analogous reasons to appraise highly religion? To be sure, it often leads to horrors and abominations, but it also yields "moral gems."[27]

If this argument is to be persuasive, however, everything turns *yet again* on questions of degree: does religious belief and practice yield valuable outcomes *often enough* relative to the bad outcomes it yields? If the National Science Foundation mostly funded work in alchemy, intelligent design, and Lamarckianism, while occasionally footing the bill for genuinely cutting-edge research in chemistry or biology, we would not highly appraise the institution but instead think its existence *barely justified* given the track record. The track record on religion is, quite obviously mixed—indeed, sufficiently mixed, that it is hard to see the kinds of considerations noted above supporting the attitude of appraisal respect.

But perhaps a much more forceful case can be made for religion as an object of appraisal respect. Such would be the import of John Finnis's bold claim that

[r]eligion deserves constitutional mention, not because it is a passionate or deep commitment, but be-

cause it is the practical expression of, or response to, truths about human society, about the persons who are a political community's members, and about the world in which any such community must take its place and find its ways and means. Even the many seriously misguided religions tell in some respects more truth about the constitution's ultimate natural (transcendent, supra-natural) foundations than any atheism or robust agnosticism can.[28]

Finnis follows Thomas Aquinas in claiming that "the rationality norms which guide us in *all* our fruitful thinking also, and integrally, summon us to affirm the existence and providence of God. . . ."[29] These are astonishing claims, which, if they could be made good, would require a wholly different approach to the law of religious liberty, as Finnis well appreciates. We must, then, ask what arguments Finnis has in support of these ambitious theses?

According to Finnis, the "norms of rational enquiry" necessary for any inquiry into reality end up leading us to a rational belief in God.[30] I quote at some length from Finnis, so as not to be accused of misrepresenting the position:

Such norms guide all scientific inquiry, all scientific discovery and all scientific achievements and applications—and are the source, equally, of all enquiry, discovery and judgment in fields which lie wholly or partly beyond the methods of natural science, fields such as mathematics, logic, philosophy, history, and the interpretation of texts and conversations. In all these fields, truth is found and knowledge of reality is won by hypothesizing (and then, when evidence and argument fail to disconfirm it, appropriately *concluding* to) some explanation, some explanatory factor or state of affairs or reality ... in preference to mere chance or inexplicable ("blind") necessity. So, one of the many rationality norms is: an adequately explanatory reason why something is so rather than otherwise is to be expected, unless one has a reason not to expect such an explanatory reason.[31]

There is a large literature on the epistemic norms operative in scientific practice,[32] but that literature is not in evidence in Finnis's discussion. No citation is given, either, for the curious proposition that it is a norm of rationality that one should *expect* an "explanatory reason" (I assume that is a *causal* reason) "why something is so rather than otherwise." To the extent we expect that phenomena have causal determinants it is because of *past experience*, because it has turned out so often (at least since the Scientific Revolution) that things that seemed inexplicable actually have causes. It is not a norm of rationality—Finnis has no account of those—that things we observe are explicable in terms of antecedent causes; it is an *inductive inference* based on past success. It is clearly defeasible, which belies its purported status as a "norm of rationality": no one is unreasonable should they conclude that a particular phenomenon is a product of chance (chance, itself, being an object of study since the scientific revolution, but put that to one side). *Norms* of rationality, one might have thought, have the feature that should you violate them you are, necessarily, *unreasonable*. But since it is reasonable—that is, since it answers to norms of rationality and evidence—to sometimes conclude that a particular phenomenon is purely a "product" of chance, it would follow that there is no "norm of rationality" at work here.

Finnis is surely right that "science progresses constantly by treating chance as the residuum of coincidence in a domain dominated by what is explicable because it is not by chance,"[33] but that is an a posteriori fortuity, not any a priori or "transcendent" (as he sometimes calls it) reality.

Finnis adduces no evidence from actual scientific practice that it is otherwise. There are not, contra Finnis, any "lines of thought that converge on the conclusion that one should affirm a transcendent cause."[34] What there is, instead, is actual scientific practice that finds that a combination of deterministic and probabilistic laws describe wide swaths of natural phenomena, and the recognition that some phenomena have no causal determinants at all.

I should emphasize that Finnis, a distinguished philosopher of law and Aquinas scholar, as well as a devout Catholic his entire adult life, represents the intellectual best that contemporary Thomism has to offer. The dogmatic incantation of "norm of rationality" functions, alas, in Thomistic discourse as a bludgeon meant to cow the opposition and vindicate the epistemic bona fides of irrational and long-discredited positions without any actual argument or evidence. The dialectical bankruptcy of Thomism, which is apparent to everyone outside the relevant sectarian group, will not, I am afraid, salvage an argument for appraisal respect of religious conscience.

Conclusion: A Nietzschean Postscript

It bears emphasizing that the argument of this chapter—that religious conscience per se is not a proper object of appraisal respect—is in no way an argument for any other propositions with which it might be confused on a superficial reading—for example, that no *particular* religion might be a proper object of appraisal respect[35]; or that religious belief per se deserves disrespect (e.g., intolerance). The last pernicious conclusion is one that is no part of the argument of the book: I have adopted throughout what seems to me the clearly correct Nietzschean posture—namely, that the *falsity* of beliefs and/or their *lack of epistemic warrant* are not necessarily objections to those beliefs; indeed, false or unwarranted beliefs are almost certainly, as Nietzsche so often says, necessary conditions of life itself, and so of considerable value, and certainly enough value to warrant toleration.

CHAPTER V

The Law of Religious Liberty in a Tolerant Society

Let us briefly recap the conclusions of the arguments of the preceding chapters. Kantian and utilitarian traditions of moral thought generate compelling support for the conclusion that the state should protect liberty of conscience under the rubric of principled toleration. But there appears to be no equally principled argument that picks out distinctively *religious* conscience as an object of special moral and legal solicitude. If *liberty of conscience* is morally important, then what should we do with respect to the extant law of religious liberty, which treats religious conscience as more important than any other kind—sometimes, as in America, de jure and always, as in every other Western democracy, de facto?

Remember, of course, what is at stake in this question. The constitutional and statutory provisions that encode religious toleration provide that individuals with claims of religious conscience can request, and sometimes secure, exemptions from generally applicable laws, an opportunity unavailable to the individual with a "merely" secular claim of conscience. Given the lack of any good moral reason for treating the nonreligious unequally with regard to claims of conscience, one obvious solution would be to extend the breadth of exemptions from generally applicable laws to all claims of conscience, religious or not. If a boy's Sikh religion requires him to bring a knife to school, then he should be eligible for an exemption from the law forbidding students from carrying potential weapons. But if another rural boy's family tradition—going back five generations, passed down from father to son as a sacred rite of passage to manhood—demands that a young man after reaching puberty must always carry his hunting knife with him, then that boy, too, should have a colorable claim for exemption from the ban on weapons in school. And what then of the lone eccentric, who for reasons known only to him, feels a categorical compulsion, with which he deeply identifies as a matter of personal integrity, to always have a knife nearby—does he, too, have a claim for exemption as a matter of liberty of conscience?

Universal Exemptions for Conscience:
Three Objections

From a principled point of view, there may be no difference among all the preceding claims of conscience,[1] but it
seems unlikely that any legal system will embrace this capacious approach to liberty of conscience that would involve according all these claims of conscience equal legal
standing. In the first instance, it would be tantamount
to constitutionalizing a right to civil disobedience,[2] a
posture it is hard to imagine any legal system adopting.
What legal system will say "this is the law, but, of course,
you have the right to disregard it on grounds of conscience"? This would appear to amount to a legalization
of anarchy!

We can cash out the import of the metaphor of "constitutionalizing civil disobedience" in terms of far more
mundane and pragmatic reasons why no legal system is
going to embrace a "constitutional right to civil disobedience" in the form of a general liberty of conscience,
whatever its pedigree or character. Claims of conscience
present hard evidential issues for courts, and their correct
resolution is important since what is at stake is the very
ability of the community to enforce its laws of general
applicability. From the epistemic standpoint, the great

virtue of claims of religious conscience is that they typically provide evidential proxies for conscience that are much easier for courts to assess. A claim of conscience is, after all, a claim about what one *must* do, no matter what—not as a matter of crass self-interest but because it is a kind of moral imperative central to one's integrity as a person, to the meaning of one's life. But how are courts to determine whether someone's claim to defy the law is *really* a claim of conscience? That is the specter that haunts any legal regime governing liberty of conscience, and the great practical advantage of a regime that privileges liberty of religious conscience is that it gives courts a more robust evidential base for their determinations. After all, a litigant who asserts a claim of religious conscience must reference a *religion*. Religions typically have texts, doctrines, and commands, either written or passed down orally among many adherents. Membership in the religion in question usually depends (as Émile Durkheim's account of religion correctly noticed[3]) on participation in *practices*, *rituals*, and *ceremonies*. All of this gives the courts a rich evidential base for assessing the genuineness of a claim of conscience. Rather than trying to peer into the depths of a man's soul, the court can simply weigh oral and textual evidence about the religion's doctrines and its requirements as well as the evidence that the claimant in question really was a member of the religion, as reflected in his participation in the relevant practice and rituals.[4]

These evidential considerations might suggest a compromise posture, short of extending exemptions from generally applicable laws to *all* claims of conscience, no matter how individual (or idiosyncratic). Recognizing the epistemic problem—that courts must adjudicate whether a claim of conscience *is really a claim of conscience*—perhaps we should simply extend legal protection for liberty of conscience *only* to claims of conscience that are rooted in communal or group traditions and practices that mimic, from an evidential point of view, those of religious groups?[5] Think of the vigorous and vocal groups now common in affluent capitalist societies that promote veganism or animal rights. Many vegans, for example, regard the appropriation and consumption (as food or otherwise) of nonhuman animals as morally odious, akin to the chattel slavery of humans.[6] Organized as these individuals are into ideological and advocacy (and even sometimes revolutionary[7]) groups, it is easy enough to find many of the same kinds of evidentiary markers of a genuine claim of conscience as in the case of a religious claimant. So why not give the vegan prisoner, with bona fide involvements in the animal liberation "movement," legal standing to claim exemption from dietary and/or prison work regimens that would violate her conscientious objection to the exploitation of nonhuman animals?

Notice, of course, that there is no principled reason for expanding exemptions this way; the proposal is motivated entirely by the practical and epistemic worries noted above. This approach would have the virtue of not treating only claims of religious conscience as legally special when there is no good moral reason to do so. But it would also have the unwelcome consequence of treating genuine claims of conscience unequally before the law, simply based on how practicable it is for courts to adjudicate their genuineness, and nothing else. Organized vegans would have legal standing, but not Henry David Thoreau or his twenty-first-century analogue.

Is the unfairness of such inequality justifiable? Should we not simply concede that the success of *any* claim at law depends on the ability to prove one's entitlement, and leave it at that?[8] Some accused are wrongfully convicted of crimes, but that does not mean that the right of criminal defendants to prove their innocence constitutes an injustice. If everyone at least has a right to establish a claim of conscience demanding an exemption, why should it matter, morally, that not everyone can prove the genuineness of his or her claim equally well (or equally easily)?

We may put the challenge even more starkly. Those innocent of a crime with which they are charged are entitled to be acquitted, and it is an injustice if they are convicted instead. But that injustice does not entail that it is unjust (because unequal) to establish a system of criminal justice administration in which defendants must try to prove their innocence. Those with a genuine claim of conscience are also entitled (in a legal regime with universal exemptions for claims of conscience) to an exemption; it is an injustice if they are denied the exemption, but that does not mean the system of universal exemptions is morally objectionable. Is there any pertinent difference between the two cases?

The difference turns, I suspect, on matters of degree regarding the ease, or difficulty, of proof. If it were extremely difficult for most of those charged with certain kinds of crimes to prove their innocence such that many innocent defendants were regularly convicted despite their lack of culpability, then a complaint about unequal treatment seems to me to have moral force. The objection then would be that the standards of proof had been calibrated in such a way to entail unequal treatment of too many defendants similarly situated in terms of culpability.

This will entail a judgment about matters of degree, to repeat, and it is possible that a scheme of universal exemptions for claims of conscience, with suitable evidential standards, might do well enough to blunt the inequality objection. In that event, the inequality of treatment of claims of conscience is not *necessarily* fatal to a scheme of universal exemptions for claims of conscience.

It bears noticing, however, that a third difficulty with such a scheme of exemptions looms, one that is quite independent of the question of proof.[9] For exemptions from generally applicable laws often impose burdens on those who have no claim of exemption. Think of mandatory military service: if those with claims of conscience against military duty are exempted from service, then the burden (and all the very serious risks) will fall upon those who either have no conscientious objection or cannot successfully establish their conscientious claim. Let us call this the Rousseauian worry about exemptions. If general compliance with laws is necessary to promote the "general welfare" or the "common good," then selective exemptions from those laws is a morally objectionable injury to the general welfare. To be sure, not every law from which exemptions might be sought will impede the lawful pursuit of the general welfare, but many will—whether it is exemptions from zoning regulations for religious institutions, exemptions from mandatory vaccination schemes, or exemptions from a ban on knives in the schools.[10] I will call such exemptions, for ease of reference, *burden-shifting exemptions*. Burden-shifting exemptions seem prima facie objectionable, even if we are confident that our standards of proof for claiming exemptions are such that no individual claimant should feel unjustly treated. So putting practical considerations to one side, there remains a moral objection (the Rousseauian worry, as I've called it) to a universal scheme of burden-shifting exemptions. On the other hand, exemptions from generally applicable laws for claims of conscience that do not impose burdens on others—such as the right to wear certain religious garb, or to use certain otherwise illegal narcotics in religious rituals[11]—might not raise the Rousseauian worry at all.

The "No Exemptions" Approach— and Its Problems

There is, to be sure, an alternative route suggested by the argument of the preceding chapters. If there is no good moral reason to treat *religious* conscience as special— indeed, no reason (except practical and evidential) to treat *communally sanctioned* claims of conscience as special—and if there are Rousseauian reasons pertaining to the general welfare for the state to enact and enforce its laws, then perhaps we should simply abandon the idea that there should be exemptions from generally applicable laws, except when no burden-shifting is involved?[12] To be sure, the state may not pass laws whose aim is to suppress claims of conscience—that would be inconsistent with principled toleration—but the state may, of course, pursue neutral objectives like the safety, health, and well-being of the populace.[13] If we are not to unfairly privilege religious claims of conscience by allowing their adherents to opt out of neutral legal requirements while nonreligious conscientious claimants must bear the burden of defeat (or sanction, should they resist), and if we are not to impede realization of the general welfare by permitting some to opt out of societal burdens, then perhaps it is time to say, the law is the law, and there will be no exemptions for claims of conscience, religious or otherwise? (This does not prejudge the possibility that sometimes civil disobedience will be the morally appropriate response to the law, but that is a different issue.)

Now, eliminating all exemptions would, as Martha Nussbaum emphasizes,[14] impose a burden on matters of minority conscience, since, for obvious reasons, societies are unlikely to create legal prohibitions that burden widely accepted demands of conscience, religious or otherwise.[15] Insofar as there are more religious claims of conscience than nonreligious claims—a distinct possibility in many societies—then imposing a No Exemptions regime will undoubtedly burden religious claims of conscience more than nonreligious ones, and will burden minority claims of conscience, religious or otherwise, more than majority claims of conscience, religious or otherwise. That certainly seems unfortunate and unfair, but is it more unfair than limiting the burden to minority claims of conscience that cannot claim any religious authority on their behalf? At least generally applicable laws *unintentionally* burden minority claims of conscience, whereas a regime of exemptions *intentionally* privileges religious claims of conscience, to the exclusion of others, even though there is no moral reason to do so. If it is liberty of conscience *simpliciter* that has moral standing, then it is hard to see the moral force of a demand for purportedly equal treatment that arbitrarily selects some subset of claims of conscience for special consideration.[16]

We can also now see quite clearly the practical import of the issue raised in chapter 4—that is, of deciding whether the moral foundation of liberty of conscience is toleration (what we there called minimal respect) or something more affirmative, like appraisal respect. Those practices that are proper objects of appraisal respect often do command exemptions from generally applicable laws. Think of the tax-exempt status of charitable (including religious) organizations in American law.[17] Because American society highly appraises charitable activities (a legal posture that has obvious ideological benefits in an economic system predicated on greed), they are exempt from the general rules pertaining to taxation. More generally, we might think that attitudes and practices that warrant appraisal respect ought to command governmental solicitude and support, as opposed to "mere" toleration. If religious claims of conscience were proper objects of appraisal respect—a thesis we rejected in chapter 4—then a broad claim for exemptions would have more force than it does. But if the only claim of conscience is for toleration, then it is not obvious why the state should subordinate its other morally important objectives—safety, health, well-being, equal treatment before the law—to claims of religious conscience.

The argument, so far, may seem to have pressed toward the No Exemptions approach to claims of conscience (or, more precisely, no exemptions for burden-shifting claims of conscience), yet surely we must bear in mind that a regime of religious toleration also demands that the state not single out particular religions for persecution or coercive burdens. To the extent burdens on conscience are incidental to the pursuit of legitimate state objectives, the No Exemptions approach poses no obstacle. But if we adopt the No Exemptions approach as a matter of fairness—because religious claims of conscience have no greater entitlement to exemptions than nonreligious claims of conscience—and because of Rousseauian concerns about the general welfare, then surely we open the door to state conduct motivated by antireligious animus, but under the pretense of legitimate, neutral objectives. Are not sectarian bias and prejudice likely to co-opt principled arguments for unprincipled ends, a concern that seems particularly acute in the domain of religious liberty?[18]

Consider the controversy over the French ban on ostentatious religious symbols—such as Muslim headscarves, or Jewish skullcaps, or large Christian crosses—in the public schools.[19] Its purpose was one arguably consistent with French *laïcité*[20]—namely, to preserve the public sphere as a secular one in which persons interact as equal citizens without regard to sectarian identities, religious or ethnic. Yet given the political context,[21] and obvious French antipathy toward Muslims (not to mention the history of French anti-Semitism), it is tempting to think of this law as a surreptitious assault on the basic protections of religious toleration. But notice—and this might seem, at first blush, the important point here—that such an assault would be effectively defeated by a legal regime that recognized religious exemptions from generally applicable laws.

Of course, it is precisely the point of the French conception of laïcité to reject such exemptions, in favor of an ideal of equal citizenry of *persons qua persons*. But more important, the real objection here is not to the absence of exemptions for claims of religious conscience from generally applicable laws but to the fact that the law in question *seems* a mere subterfuge for a morally impermissible motive or purpose—namely, the motive or purpose of *not* tolerating a particular religion, namely, Islam. If there are good moral arguments for liberty of conscience—precisely the view defended in chapter 1—then those arguments must surely rule out the persecution of particular claims of religious conscience not because they are religious but because they are claims of conscience. The only question about the French law banning headscarves, then, is whether it is animated by intolerance toward Islam, not whether it reflects the drawbacks of a system that lacks exemptions for claims of religious conscience.

Can we dismiss the preceding concerns quite so easily? The argument for liberty of conscience, to repeat, demands toleration of claims of conscience, but the No

Exemptions approach says that the law need not carve out exemptions from generally applicable laws for all claims of conscience (except perhaps those that do not involve pernicious burden-shifting). The worry, then, is that the requirement of toleration will amount to little in practice. Could not the state simply burden *any* disfavored claim of conscience under the guise of pursuing a general objective? In the case of French laïcité, the problem is even worse than that, since the general objective in question is one that is *not* neutral about religion but specifically deems religious attributes ones that do not belong in the public sphere. Is not exclusion from the public sphere in this manner itself a pernicious *burden*?

It is important to keep the two issues separate. One worry (the focus so far) is that a No Exemptions approach makes it too easy for states to burden conscience under the guise of pursuing neutral objectives. The second (and new) worry is that the objective of excluding religion from the public sphere (in the manner of French laïcité) is, itself, inherently intolerant, and so impermissible.

The first worry raises only an epistemic or evidential issue. After all, it has been the baseline premise of the argument of this book that, *of course*, state action whose aim is to burden particular religious claims of conscience is inconsistent with the moral requirement of toleration! Any prohibition, in any area of law, on particular state purposes will raise evidential questions about how to identify cases where the forbidden purpose is really at work. On its face it seems odd to think that the correct response to an evidential problem is an exemption from the law that is not otherwise morally justified. To be sure, if we thought the evidential problem were insurmountable—that is, if we had reason to think that it will be impossibly difficult to discriminate between the *facade* of neutral purpose and *actual* neutral purpose in legislation that burdens religion—then we might think exemptions for religious claims of conscience the preferable approach, notwithstanding the inequality such an approach entails and notwithstanding the burden on the general welfare. But notice that this style of argument could equally well propel us back to general exemptions for claims of conscience, to the extent we thought the facade of neutral purpose could regularly cover over the attempt to persecute nonreligious claims of conscience as well.

What, then, of the second worry? Is French laïcité in its very nature impermissibly intolerant by excluding religion from the public sphere?[22] Does not the legal judgment that, in the public square, the equality of persons qua persons demands that they shed the visible indicia of their religious identities constitute intolerance of religion inconsistent with the arguments of chapter 1? The immediate answer might seem to be "no," since the Rawlsian and Millian arguments of chapter 1 only established that there is a good moral case for liberty of conscience, not that such liberty could only be realized in the public arena. It is one thing for the state to criminalize a particular religion and its practice, quite another for the state to say that the religion and its practices do not belong in the public schools. Is not my liberty of conscience intact if I may proselytize my neighbors and teach my children the purported truths of dialectical materialism or Hayekian free market utopianism, for example, even though I may not usurp the public school curriculum for the same philosophical program?

Of course, that is not quite the burden involved in French laïcité. The more precise analogue would be the situation in which the state declares that one may not even act or dress in such a way in the public schools as to evince one's allegiance to the forbidden ideologies, whether Islam or Christianity, Leninism or Hayekianism. No headscarves, no skullcaps, no ostentatious crosses, and no hammer-and-sickle or "greed is good" T-shirts: *that* would constitute the relevantly analogous regulation. Would such a prohibition constitute impermissible intolerance?

What *Precisely* Does Toleration Require?

This question brings to the fore an important issue so far unaddressed explicitly in the argument of this book. The intolerant want to "stamp out" disfavored beliefs and practices, and we have adduced, in chapter 1, moral arguments against intolerance (limited, of course, by the Harm Principle). But is the protection against intolerance exhausted by a mere prohibition on annihilation or imprisonment of those with the disfavored beliefs and practices? Does the state discharge its obligation of toleration if it simply refrains from murdering or jailing those in the grips of "disreputable" claims of conscience? Surely there are other ways for a state to be intolerant, but this gets us to the real challenge posed by French laïcité.

Let us shift our focus, for a moment, from religion to political speech. France, like many European countries, imposes legal restrictions on public (and even private) advocacy of and displays of Nazism.[23] Wearing Nazi regalia in the public schools, or anywhere in public, would quite clearly incur legal sanction in most of the countries that survived the horrors of the Nazi era. These laws are quite clearly "intolerant" of Nazism and, equally clearly, they infringe on matters of conscience, albeit matters of depraved conscience. One need only recall Adolf Hitler's conduct toward the end of World War II—when he insisted on diverting manpower and resources to the extermination of the Jews rather than freeing the manpower up to fight the war and utilizing the Jews as slave labor[24]—to realize that he was a "man of principle" in the simple sense that he pursued the objectives he thought morally correct and obligatory, notwithstanding the consequences. Moral philosophers have recently called attention to the extent to which the street-level perpetrators of Nazi horrors were men (and sometime women) of conscience, also acting in accordance with their sense, however warped, of moral duty.[25]

If people act on the basis of their "Nazi conscience," does liberty of conscience require us to acquiesce? It quite obviously does not, for reasons that were emphasized in chapter 1—namely, that a principle of toleration operates under the side-constraints imposed by something like the Harm Principle.[26] The state is under no moral obligation to tolerate acts of conscience that cause harm to other persons. But that does not get us very far with the current question, since typical European restrictions on "Nazi speech" are blanket bans on *speech and symbols*, not simply on actions. The European legal restrictions on even the *expression* of Nazism reflect some combination of the judgments that: (1) such expressions run too great a risk of harm to humans, and (2) Nazism is akin to the denial of geometrical truths (to borrow the preferred Millian analogy[27])—that is, it represents a set of ideas about which, to quote John Stuart Mill, "there is nothing at all to be said on the wrong side of the question. The peculiarity of the evidence . . . is that all the argument is on one side,"[28] which is to say: *not* the Nazi side. I shall refer to the first consideration justifying a limitation on liberty of conscience as the "risk of harm" consideration; and I shall refer to the second as the "falsehoods need not be heard" consideration (though really we are talking only about *clear* or *obvious* or *indisputable* falsehoods). Does either consideration have any bearing on whether a regime like French laïcité constitutes morally impermissible intolerance of religion?

The actually existing French regime of laïcité obviously cannot be justified on the grounds that falsehoods need not be heard, since that would require a much more far-reaching set of restrictions on religious expression that go well beyond the desire to preserve the public sphere as one in which citizens interact as equal citizens, without regard to sectarian identities. If burdens on Islamic headscarves and Jewish skullcaps were to be justified on the grounds that falsehoods need not be heard, then Catholic churches, Islamic mosques, and Jewish synagogues would obviously need to be shut down as well, and Bibles, Korans, and Torahs would need to be confiscated, but that is no part of the program of French laïcité.[29]

That means the only colorable defense of French laïcité, from the standpoint of principled toleration, is one based on risk-of-harm considerations. If religious expression is to be treated like Nazi expression in the public sphere (consistently with the constraints imposed by the principle of toleration), then it must be because the risk of harm associated with religious expression is on a par with the risk (if not the harm) associated with religious expression. It bears emphasizing at this point that there are two components to what is at issue here: the risk *and* the harm. The harm in question is the transformation of the public sphere from one in which persons interact qua persons to one in which they interact on the basis of religious identities. That risk is *very real*, as experience in the United States would suggest—where, for example, the vast majority of the population reports that they would never vote for an atheist for elective office but express much higher levels of tolerance for (i.e., willingness to support for elective office) gay men and lesbians, Muslims, and Jews.[30] But even in the United States this antipathy toward atheism does not manifest itself (at least not yet) in the burnings of heretics or the legal persecution of nonbelievers. Yet lesser, but still real, harms are apparent from the hyperreligiosity of the United States, such as the assault on science curricula in the public schools. (As I will argue below, the state can, quite consistently with principled toleration, disestablish religion from the public schools.)

Remember that the moral magnitude of the harm still remains at issue. No one doubts that those in thrall to Nazi claims of conscience will act, to the extent they can, in ways that really harm human beings. The harm at issue in the case of religious invasion of the public sphere is far different: not ordinarily to physical well-being, but, in the first instance, to a moral ideal of equal citizenship. The denial, de facto if not de jure, of full equal citizenship might lead to more tangible blood-and-flesh harms, but the prediction that it will do so is considerably more speculative, and not obviously adequate to support a Harm Principle argument in the spirit of Mill (even allowing for the ambiguities of what constitutes "harm" in a Millian framework). The only risk of harm to which the French approach can reliably advert is the risk of increased false belief, but that, as we have already seen in chapter 4, is not obviously a harm, since false beliefs often have salutary effects (they are, as Nietzsche says, sometimes conditions of life itself), both for their adherents and sometimes for others.

The conclusion, then, seems clear: French laïcité (at least as made concrete in legislation like the ban on ostentatious religious symbols in the schools) is, in fact, a case of impermissible intolerance of religion unless one were to assume, contrary to reality, that most religions burdened by it were akin to Nazism. But that also means that the No Exemptions approach to principled toleration is incompatible with a regime like that of French laïcité. In fact, this should not be a surprising conclusion, since the central contention of the No Exemptions approach is that there do not need to be exemptions for claims of conscience from laws *with neutral objectives.* The "neutrality" of objectives required, it now seems, requires neutrality as to dictates of conscience that do not violate the Harm Principle.[31] Since it cannot be maintained that religious dictates of conscience *in general* violate the Harm Principle, a general ban on the expressions of such claims of conscience in the public sphere cannot be justified. (More carefully tailored bans on particular claims of religious conscience might be justified, but that is a different question.) It is not enough for toleration of conscience that the state not jail or annihilate the adherents of the disfavored claims of conscience; the state must also not directly target or coercively burden their claims of conscience, unless they run afoul of the Harm Principle—more precisely, unless they pose risk of harm or constitute falsehoods that need not be heard. These points, however, are no objection to the No Exemptions approach except in the unusual circumstances in which we think the *evidential* question about whether the state is really pursuing permissible, neutral purposes cannot be answered—in which case the default position would be suspicion of any law that burdens conscience. But that does not appear to be our world—at least not yet—and so the No Exemptions approach stands, even if it is not compatible with French laïcité.

Religious Toleration and Religious Establishment

Our primary focus so far has been on the interaction between the requirements of a principle of toleration and exemptions from generally applicable laws that infringe on claims of conscience—what, in the United States, would be known as "free exercise" issues. But any conception of religious liberty must also address issues of religious *establishment*—that is, issues about the state endorsement of a particular religion, or of religion as against nonreligion, or even of nonreligion as against religion. How does religious establishment interact with religious liberty and, in particular, with the moral requirements imposed by a principle of toleration? It bears emphasizing that I will not be developing a *general* theory of religious establishment here but asking *only* what limits on religious establishment are established by the demand to tolerate liberty of conscience, including religious conscience. *It is clear that religious establishment also implicates equality values*, but I will not be considering those in the discussion that follows. Even if the establishment of religion or nonreligion is compatible with principled toleration (as I will argue), it may prove incompatible with equality values. I postpone full consideration of that question for a different occasion.

We have already broached aspects of the establishment issue through the preceding discussion of French laïcité. French laïcité represents a particular kind of disestablishment of religion, excluding, as it has in recent years, religious expression and symbols from much of the public sphere—an exclusion that, as I have argued above, cannot be justified on Harm Principle grounds, and thus seems to constitute a burden on conscience inconsistent with principled toleration. But it does not follow from this that disestablishment of religion in favor of nonreligion is inconsistent with principled toleration. After all, liberal states necessarily disestablish all illiberal claims of conscience by putting the imprimatur of the state on equality, on democracy, on liberty, and so on—though they do not go the intolerant step further of forbidding all expression in the public sphere of illiberal ideas, except when those ideas are likely (perhaps imminently likely) to result in actions that violate the Harm Principle.

Yet most liberal states go a step beyond that, also putting the imprimatur of the state, for example, on science as a reliable source of knowledge about the natural world, as reflected in the curricula of the public schools, or by using public monies to fund medical research and procedures to which some taxpayers object "as a matter of conscience."[32] I shall argue that, consistent with a principle of toleration, the state may indeed put its imprimatur on values and worldviews that are inconsistent with the claims of conscience of some of its citizens (as long as its objective in doing so is *not* to suppress or coercively burden those claims of conscience but to achieve some conception of the good—a point to which we shall return). The state, consistent with the principle of toleration, may even disestablish religion, though not in the manner of recent French laïcité. These conclusions will no doubt be congenial to other religion skeptics, but it bears emphasizing that the arguments apply equally well in a different direction: nothing in the *principle of toleration* is incompatible with state establishment of religion, as long as it is done in such a way that it does not burden nonreligious claims of conscience—except, of course, to the extent that such coercive burdens can be justified on Harm Principle grounds (either because of the risk of harm or because of the falsehoods need not be heard rationales[33]).

Let us start with establishment of religion. Many Western democracies, such as those of the United Kingdom and Germany, have established religions, and yet have robust regimes of liberty of conscience in which a range of moral and political views find expression in the public sphere that are unknown in countries like the United States, which do not establish any religion. (Such natural experiments should perhaps serve as cautionary notes to anyone who thinks a legal regime plays a significant causal role in constituting the moral culture of a nation.) What we learned from consideration of the case of French laïcité is that establishment of what I will call henceforth "a Vision of the Good"—a vision, broadly speaking, of what is worthwhile or important[34]—is compatible with toleration as long as it does not have as its purpose to burden coercively minority claims of conscience, beyond what would be licensed by the Harm Principle. The problem with the recent interpretations of French laïcité is that they try to establish a particular Vision of the Good—of persons as equal *qua* persons, without regard to religion or ethnicity—through coercion of those with minority claims of religious conscience, and in a way that cannot be justified on Harm Principle grounds. Religious symbols worn by students in the public schools simply do not undermine democratic equality, except on assumptions about human psychology and sociology not borne out by present realities in the secular democracies, and that is true even if the French state might be quite justified, consistent with a principle of toleration, in, for example, suppressing the hate speech of an Imam who claimed that all non-Muslims were infidels who should be murdered.[35] Without a doubt, it would be consistent with principled toleration for the French government to teach secularism in the public schools, to affirm the secular character of the republic in its public pronouncements, and to allocate its resources in a way consistent with these objectives. What it cannot do, consistent with principled toleration, is try to shut down private citizens who would express a different Vision of the Good.

British establishment of Anglicanism provides the natural counterpoint to French laïcité, as an example of an establishment of a *religious* Vision of the Good that does not impinge on the principle of toleration.[36] Anglican Christianity is the "official" religion of Britain—it is literally "the Church of England"—and this means Anglican prayers and liturgies are customary features of public life, and at least the royal family still professes allegiance to the church. But no one can doubt that modern Britain adheres to principled toleration when it comes to other religions: there are no religious tests for the holding of public office; sectarian religious schools in non-Anglican traditions actually receive public funding; other religious traditions are guaranteed the right to practice their religions; and no non-Anglican religious practices are criminalized or otherwise suppressed. Perhaps this is a peculiar artifact of English culture—after all, as my English friends like to point out, it is not entirely clear that the Archbishop of Canterbury even believes in God—but even so, it is a clear case of religious establishment that seems fully compatible with the requirements of toleration of nonestablished religions.

If religious establishment can be compatible with principled toleration, so too can religious disestablishment, as long as it does not target for suppression or coercive burdens religious or nonreligious claims of conscience—except, to repeat, when warranted by the Harm Principle.

The state may endorse a Vision of the Good according to which religious explanations for the origin of human life are mythologies that have no place in the public schools, but what they may not do is prevent the creationists and intelligent design proponents from articulating those views in private and in public (if not in the state schools). The French state could even endorse the ideal of citizens interacting as equals qua citizens, without regard to race or religious or ethnicity, but what it cannot do is prevent citizens from displaying their religious convictions in public (as little as it would be justified in preventing them from displaying their ethnicity or race in public).

There will remain, to be sure, fuzzy boundary cases involved in the idea that the state may endorse a Vision of the Good but not suppress the expression of contrary visions. Some state endorsements may crowd out private expressions of contrary visions, for example—a worry that may be especially serious where the media of communication are under state control. (On the other hand, Britain is, again, a counterexample to this concern.) But even allowing for hard cases, it seems clear that, in principle, there is no incompatibility between state endorsement of a Vision of the Good—religious or irreligious—and the demands of principled toleration.[37] Principled toleration requires the state not to persecute or target for special burdens particular claims of conscience; it does not require the state to cease being a state—that is, to cease promoting a Vision of the Good, of the public good, social welfare, or human fulfillment.[38]

American constitutional law has recently confronted a version of this problem in the context of the "viewpoint discrimination" revolution in Establishment Clause jurisprudence. The U.S. Supreme Court had, for some time, interpreted the constitutional prohibition on an "establishment" of religion as forbidding laws requiring "excessive entanglement" with religion.[39] The meaning of that prohibition was also, for a generation or so, moderately clear: it meant that state-supported schools could not, for example, let their facilities be utilized by sectarian religious groups promoting a sectarian, religious message. This was a kind of disestablishment: it said that state schools were off limits to those who would promote religion. This disestablishment coexisted, of course, with secure protections for both religious expression in private life and the advocacy of religious claims in other public forums, such as through the media and the proverbial "public square."

In the 1980s, conservative religious groups began litigating against such prohibitions, arguing that they were unconstitutional "viewpoint discrimination" by the state:

if state schools open their after-school facilities or otherwise offer support to various viewpoints (e.g., the animal rights group, or the College Republicans, or the local chapter of the Socialist Workers Party), then it is an unconstitutional violation of freedom of *speech* to prohibit religious groups from utilizing those facilities *on the grounds that their viewpoint is religious.*[40] But if the preceding argument of this chapter is correct, then disestablishment of religion by barring the use of public schools by religious groups is morally consistent with principled toleration.[41] The state can establish a Vision of the Good that does not include religion, meaning that state schools need not accommodate religious expression, contrary to the wrong turn taken by the U.S. Supreme Court; what the state cannot do, consistent with a principle of toleration, is deny individuals the opportunity to express in other aspects of their life a religiously grounded Vision of the Good.

But what precisely is the difference between saying, "You may not use public school facilities to teach a particular religious dogma" and saying, "You may not appear in a public school wearing clothing that reflects your religious beliefs"? After all, French laïcité targets the latter, as well as the former, but now it appears we are claiming there is a morally pertinent difference between the cases. And, indeed, there is, though, as in all these cases, some of the differences are ones of degree, rather than kind. The argument so far has been that the state must, of course, express a Vision of the Good, and that it can do so consistent with principled toleration as long as its aim is not to suppress or coercively burden individual claims of conscience. But why does it constitute an impermissible burden on my religious Vision of the Good to forbid me from wearing a Jewish skullcap in the public schools, but it does not constitute any such burden to forbid me from teaching the truths of the Torah in the public schools?

If states can—indeed, must—promote visions of the good, then they must be able to manifest their endorsement of that vision. One way in which all states do so is through their educational systems, and through what can and cannot be taught to the students in the system. Suppose a particular sect believed that the sun revolves around the earth, and that it would offend the dignity of God, who made humankind in his image, to claim otherwise. If the state turns its science classrooms over to the teaching of this view—even as one view among many that students might consider—it would, on any reasonable interpretation, undermine its endorsement of the Copernican vision of the solar system.[42] Words matter, and words spoken by agents of the state matter, at least insofar as they communicate, quite clearly, the Vision of the Good the state endorses.

But suppose our anti-Copernican sect issued a distinctive shirt to its adherents—say, one with a picture of the solar system with the earth in the center. If the state permits students in the public schools to wear that shirt, would anyone reasonably infer that the state endorses the anti-Copernican vision of the world? It is hard to see how that conclusion would be warranted, when the school as a whole—its curriculum, its books, and its facilities—are given over to teaching the Copernican conception.[43]

This argument depends, of course, on background assumptions about the significance of different forms of expression, verbal and sartorial. One could imagine local cultural norms sufficiently different from ours such that if the public schools permitted someone to appear wearing a Jewish skullcap, it was tantamount to the state endorsing Judaism. But at least in the Western democracies that does not appear to be the status quo with respect to our background norms. Conversely, one could imagine a society in which cultural norms view the public schools not as the agents of state endorsement but as akin to public parks, and so the fact that after-school facilities were turned over to the anti-Copernicans would not in any way be inconsistent with the state's endorsement of the

Copernican vision. Any plausible conception of which regulations impermissibly *coerce* or *burden* claims of conscience must be similarly attuned to local cultural norms and the factual context.[44]

It may be worth pausing to consider the contrary scenario to the American one *prior to* the "viewpoint discrimination" revolution—that is, a scenario in which the state, instead of disestablishing religion in the public schools, endorses a particular religion (say, Catholicism) and thus declines to let funding for public education be utilized for supporting Hinduism or atheism. Thus, in this alternative scenario, public school facilities would be available to the Catholic Student Society, but not to the Hindus or the atheists or perhaps even to the Republicans![45] Can a state promote a Catholic Vision of the Good this way consistent with the demands of principled toleration?

Let us assume that the background cultural norms are the same, in the sense that public schools that permit students to wear sectarian clothing of any kind are not understood to endorse that sect, and in which the content of the public school curriculum, by contrast, is generally understood to reflect the state's endorsement of a Vision of the Good. And let us suppose that our counterfactual society permits the public expression of

Hinduism, atheism, Calvinism—indeed, permits parents to send their children to appropriate sectarian schools in lieu of the public schools; indeed, in the manner of Britain, funds these "alternative" schools. It is hard to see how such a society could be deemed to run afoul of the requirements of principled toleration.[46]

The U.S. Supreme Court has often emphasized, quite reasonably, the "coercive" effect on children of certain practices in the public schools,[47] a worry wholly consistent with the earlier emphasis on local cultural norms in assessing the burdensome impact of particular regulations. But informal social norms are all important in this context. I am reminded of a story my father, now in his late seventies, told me. Raised in a moderately religious Jewish family, he became, notwithstanding, an atheist as a child and yet was subjected to years of public schooling—in Brooklyn, no less during the 1930s and '40s—in which daily readings and prayers from the King James Bible were common. Perhaps my father was sui generis, but it was not as if New York City became a center of Protestant revivalism in the 1950s and '60s among former Jews. I think the explanation is obvious: the whole cultural context of these ludicrous Bible-reading rituals was guaranteed to undermine their impact. And it was not just the public schools, but the public culture of the nation as a whole that was in-your-face Protestant. Yet it all had no impact on the liberty of conscience of a youngster in New York City, where it was easier to find Trotskyites to discuss ideas with than it was to find Baptists.

What, then, of the same youngster in Texas or Arkansas? The problem in those cases was surely the interaction of the state endorsement of religion with the local cultural norms: the dominance of Protestantism in the communities, the oppressive homogeneity of the public culture, the rhetoric of politicians and community leaders, all would serve to reinforce the message of the Bible reading, and so would turn what was slightly ludicrous and irrelevant in Brooklyn in the 1930s into something perniciously coercive. To be sure, that means if we are looking for a *national* standard for what is permissible in the public schools, then the default position, required by principled toleration, is one in which Bible readings are off limits, even if today, as then, there will be communities in which the effect of such a practice would be to encourage irreligion and ridicule of religion. So while establishment of religion or irreligion can both be compatible with principled toleration, assessing whether it is so will require case-by-case judgments in light of the prevailing cultural norms of the communities affected.

It is important to emphasize at this stage in the argument that whether we should prefer a state that establishes Catholicism or Hinduism rather than atheism is a *wholly separate moral question*. The argument so far has only been that such establishments *can* be compatible with principled toleration. One might think that establishment of a Vision of the Good, religious or irreligious, ought to turn on whether that vision is a proper object of appraisal respect. As we learned in chapter 4, however, religion *per se* is not a likely candidate for appraisal respect, which might be a fatal obstacle to defending any kind of religious establishment *even if* such establishment were compatible with principled toleration.[48] I have not, admittedly, made the argument that irreligion, in the form of atheism or otherwise, is in fact a proper object of appraisal respect, and so nothing in the preceding argument should be taken to have made the case for the establishment of irreligion either. All I have shown, if the argument has been convincing, is that religious establishment and religious disestablishment can both be compatible, under the right conditions, with principled toleration.

I have also not argued that religious establishment or disestablishment is necessarily compatible with other values, such as equality. It is possible that a religious or irreligious establishment reduces citizens with differing views to a second-class status that offends egalitarian values, and thus is objectionable on those grounds.[49] Since every state establishes a Vision of the Good—through its constitutions, its laws, and the public pronouncements of its leaders—it seems to me that there is always a risk that dissenters from that vision will feel burdened. But it is a separate question, requiring a similarly culturally nuanced inquiry, to ascertain when such establishments really offend the requirements of political equality. Only if one believed, as the Rawlsian political liberals purport to do, that there are visions everyone can accept might one think this problem can be avoided. Since the political liberals typically denominate as "unreasonable" all dissenters, this does not strike me as a theoretically interesting option.

A Final Rejoinder to the No Exemptions Approach: There Are *Only* Religious Claims of Conscience

So far I have pressed the proposition that the No Exemptions approach to claims of conscience (or at least to claims of conscience that are burden-shifting), religious or otherwise, is the one most consistent with fairness (given the practicalities of enforcement), and with the necessity for states to endorse a Vision of the Good. But a final worry no doubt looms, for are not religious claims of conscience especially resilient and fierce, especially likely to provoke backlash, disobedience, and the proverbial "blood in the streets"? After all, if your sense of categorical obligation—the hallmark of a claim of conscience—is also conjoined with concern for the well-being of your soul—not just now or tomorrow but *for all eternity*—then you will not accept interference with your obligations lightly. In short, perhaps the real reason to think that principled toleration of religious claims of conscience deserve special consideration is because they are the ones least likely to accede to a No Exemptions regime?

A suitable response to this worry must start by remembering that it is not the case that the "eternal well-being of the soul" is a *distinctive aspect* of religious categorical commands—some religious sects emphasize that, some do not. So the worry that categorical commands will, necessarily, be taken more seriously by the religious than the nonreligious cannot be right. Indeed, the whole idea that categorical demands are taken more seriously by the religious is one we rejected, effectively, in chapter 2. Recall that if one looks at horrifically

oppressive political environments, like Nazi Germany
in the 1930s—environments that would seem well-
positioned as "natural experiments" for weeding out *real*
claims of conscience (ones experienced as categorical)
from the pretenders (that is, those who relinquish their
"obligations" in the face of drastic consequences)—what
one finds is that religious believers are among those who
"risk everything" to do what is right, but so too are many
nonreligious believers such as communists. That certain
human beings are capable of experiencing certain demands as categorical is an important psychological fact
about creatures like us, to which law must be sensitive.
That psychological fact, however, does not track religious
belief.

So the initial worry should really be different: not that
religious believers will respond to a No Exemptions approach with "blood in the streets," but that in any society
there will be some conscientious individuals who will not
comply with generally applicable laws that offend their
conscience. That seems right, but it constitutes no argument against the No Exemptions approach. We can as
little justify exemptions from generally applicable laws
to "those most likely to make trouble" as we can justify
exemptions from those laws to "those who have religious
claims of conscience." Sometimes those with claims of

religious conscience may be quite correct to resist the law, but that is wholly independent of the question of whether the law ought to exempt them from its application. It has been the argument of this book that principled toleration does not require that we do so. Toleration may be a virtue, both in individuals and in states, but its selective application to the conscience of only religious believers is not morally defensible.

NOTES

Preface and Acknowledgments

1. The later Rawls also thinks that a "liberal" state cannot respect its citizens if it does not justify itself in terms that all "reasonable" citizens with differing comprehensive views can nonetheless accept. Since there are no views acceptable to all "reasonable" citizens—unless one denominates as unreasonable anyone who isn't a political liberal in basically the Rawlsian mode—it would seem that the kind of "respect" Rawls imagines isn't a live option in the real world.

Chapter I
Toleration

1. U.S. C. amend. I. Before *Employment Div., Dep't of Human Resources of Or. v. Smith*, 494 U.S. 872 (1990), courts, in assessing claims for exemptions under the Free Exercise Clause, at least nominally applied strict scrutiny to laws that burdened a sincere religious practice. *See Sherbert v. Verner*, 374 U.S. 398, 406 (1963); Michael W. McConnell, "Free Exercise Revisionism and the *Smith* Decision," *University of Chicago*

Law Review 57 (1990): 1110. That is, courts would only uphold a law that burdened such a religious belief or practice when the law served a "compelling" governmental purpose and used the least burdensome means possible in furthering that purpose. McConnell, "Free Exercise," 1110. The U.S. Supreme Court's *Smith* decision dispensed with strict scrutiny review for Free Exercise Clause claims; the Free Exercise Clause, the Supreme Court wrote, does not exempt an individual from a "valid and neutral law of general applicability" simply because the law conflicts with that individual's religion. *Smith*, 494 U.S., 880.

Congress reacted to the *Smith* ruling by passing the Religious Freedom Restoration Act of 1993 (RFRA), which reinstated strict scrutiny review of laws burdening religion. 42 U.S.C. § 2000bb. In *City of Boerne v. Flores*, 521 U.S. 507 (1997), the U.S. Supreme Court held that Congress exceeded the scope of its powers under § 5 of the Fourteenth Amendment in passing the RFRA, and that the act was thus unconstitutional, at least as applied to state and local governments. See *Cutter v. Wilkinson*, 544 U.S. 709, 733 n. 2 (2005) (noting that, while a number of circuit courts had found the RFRA constitutional with respect to the federal government, the Court had not yet addressed the issue). Congress then passed the Religious Land Use and Institutionalized Persons Act (RLUIPA) in 2000, which reinstated strict scrutiny for government regulation with respect to land use and institutions (such as prisons) which burdened religion. 42 U.S.C. § 2000cc. RLUIPA limited its scope to programs receiving federal assistance, regulations affecting interstate commerce, and individualized government assessments of proposed land uses. § 2000cc(a)(2). The Court upheld RLUIPA's constitutionality with respect to the Establishment Clause in *Cutter*, but did not address whether

Congress exceeded the scope of its powers under § 5 of the Fourteenth Amendment in passing RLUIPA, as it did with the RFRA. See 544 U.S. 709.

Many state legislatures, in response to the invalidation of the federal RFRA with respect to state and local entities in *Flores*, enacted state-level Religious Freedom Restoration Acts. Christopher C. Lund, "Religious Liberty after *Gonzales*: A Look at State RFRAs," *South Dakota Law Review* 55 (2010): 477 ("Sixteen states have now passed RFRAs"); see, e.g., the Illinois Religious Freedom Restoration Act, 1998 Ill. Legis. Serv. 90-806 (West), codified at 775 Ill. Comp. Stat. 35/1–99 (2010) (instituting the strict scrutiny, or "compelling government interest" test).

As an aside, it might be worth noting that, after *Smith*, Congress also passed the American Indian Religious Freedom Act Amendment of 1994, which legalized the religious use of peyote by Native Americans—precisely the practice that gave rise to the *Smith* suit in the first place. Pub. L. No. 103-344, 108 Stat. 3125 (1994) (codified at 42 U.S.C. § 1996a [2010]). As my research assistant John Wasserman, University of Chicago Law School class of 2012, quite aptly put it, "Congress apparently had a scorched-earth attitude toward *Smith*."

2. Grundgesetz für die Bundesrepublik Deutschland [Constitution] art. 4(1)–(2) (F.R.G.)

3. Canadian Charter of Rights and Freedoms, Part I of the Constitution Act, 1982, being Schedule B to the Canada Act 1982, ch. 11 (U.K.), § 2.

4. Article 18 of the Universal Declaration of Human Rights, G.A. Res. 217A, 71, U.N. GAOR, 3d Sess., 1st plen. mtg., U.N. Doc. A/810 (Dec. 10, 1948).

5. Some U.S. Supreme Court cases, involving constitutional challenges to the Universal Military Training and Service Act, have

moved in the direction (at least for "conscientious objectors" to military service) of expanding the meaning of "religion" to encompass broader commitments of conscience. See esp. *United States v. Seeger*, 380 U.S. 163 (1965); *Welsh v. United States*, 398 U.S. 333 [1970]. Even these cases, however, were framed as a matter of statutory interpretation, not constitutional principle. As José Louis Martí points out to me, Spanish courts have reached similar conclusions about conscientious objection to military service. In a related vein, the European Commission on Human Rights, in *Arrowsmith v. United Kingdom*, 3 E.H.R.R. 218 (1978), considered the question whether Article 9 of the European Convention, and its protection for liberty of conscience and religion, prohibits punishing a nonreligious pacifist for distributing literature to British soldiers encouraging them not to fight in Northern Ireland. The commission held that while "pacifism as a philosophy ... falls within the ambit of the right to freedom of thought and conscience" (228), it found that the literature in question did not, in fact, endorse pacifism, and so the conviction for distributing it did not violate Article 9 (230).

6. Douglas Laycock, "Regulatory Exemptions of Religious Behavior and the Original Understanding of the Establishment Clause," *Notre Dame Law Review* 81 (June 2006): 1839, notes that "the great majority of conscientious objectors . . . are traditionally religious." A substantial majority of conscientious objector cases that have appeared before the European Court of Human Rights also involve religious objectors, as opposed to those who object for secular or pacifistic reasons. See the collection of cases listed at http://www.strasbourgconsortium .org/cases.php?page_id=10#portal.case.table.php?topic=57.

My research assistant, John Wasserman, reviewed hundreds of U.S. cases brought by atheists or agnostics, and none involved challenges to "valid and neutral laws of general applicability," as Justice Antonin Scalia wrote for the majority in *Employment Div., Dep't of Human Resources of Or. v. Smith*, 494 U.S. 872, 880 (1990). Both before and since *Smith*, atheist or agnostic plaintiffs have argued that a state action violated the Free Exercise Clause *in conjunction with* the Establishment Clause or with some statute preventing preference of one sect over others (or over none). See, e.g., *Friedman v. Bd. of County Comm'rs of Bernalillo Cty.*, 781 F.2d 777 (10th Cir. 1985) (plaintiff, an atheist, argued that a county seal that featured a cross and the saying "With This We Conquer" violated the Free Exercise and Establishment Clauses). That is, atheist and agnostic plaintiffs' Free Exercise claims have not asserted that laws intended as a general reflection of religion-neutral policy somehow impinge upon their religious (or perhaps more appropriately, nonreligious) practice; rather, they involve the claim that laws are in fact not intended generally at all, but are instead laws that favor religion or particular religions over atheism or agnosticism. See, e.g., *Nicholson v. Bd. of Comm'rs of the Ala. Bar Ass'n*, 338 F. Supp. 48 (D.C. Ala. 1972) (in which the plaintiff, an atheist lawyer, challenged the state bar association's requirement that new lawyers swear an oath invoking God's name). There are, at best, only a handful of cases in which nonreligious plaintiffs were, arguably, making a claim of conscience for exemption from a generally applicable rule. So, for example, *Wells v. City and County of Denver*, 257 F.3d 1132 (10th Cir. 2001) involved a challenge by an atheist group that wanted to display a winter solstice sign in spite of a ban on private, unattended displays in a particular area. The local government had erected a holiday display featuring imagery from multiple religions; arguably, the free exercise claims put forth by the plaintiffs could be framed as a claim that the private sign ban *in that spot* infringed upon their free exercise rights. More plausibly, however, the group was challenging the religious neutrality of the display, which featured Judeo-Christian imagery—that is, the case was an Establishment Clause claim, with a Free Exercise Clause claim merely tacked on. Accordingly, the court dispensed with the Free Exercise claim in a brief paragraph, referring to the claim as "somewhat elusive." *Wells v. City and County of Denver*, 1152.

In sum, while it is arguable in a few cases that atheists or agnostics brought challenges to neutral, generally applicable laws for burdening their "religious practice," it appears as if there is no clear instance of an atheist or agnostic challenging "valid and neutral laws of general applicability." Overwhelmingly, if not universally, Establishment or Free Exercise Clause challenges to statutes or government actions by atheists or agnostics involve claims of underlying religious motives rather than claims of general motives that nonetheless unconstitutionally burden atheism or agnosticism. See, e.g., *Freedom From Religion Foundation v. Hanover School Dist.*, 2010 WL 4540588 (1st Cir., Nov. 12, 2010) (challenging the words "under God" in the Pledge of Allegiance).

7. See, e.g., Douglas Laycock on the American constitutional experience: "[I]n history that was recent to the American Founders, governmental attempts to suppress disapproved religious views had caused vast human suffering in Europe and in England and similar suffering on a smaller scale in the colonies that became the United States." Douglas Laycock, "Religious Liberty as Liberty," *Journal of Contemporary Legal Issues* 7 (1996): 317.

8. Bernard Williams, "Toleration: An Impossible Virtue?" in *Toleration: An Elusive Virtue*, ed. David Heyd (Princeton, N.J.: Princeton University Press, 1996), 19.

9. Jeremy Waldron, "Locke: Toleration and the Rationality of

Persecution," in *Justifying Toleration: Conceptual and Historical Perspectives*, ed. Susan Mendus (Cambridge: Cambridge University Press, 1988), 61–86. Waldron's reading is not uncontroversial; see, e.g., Alex Tuckness, "Locke's Main Argument for Toleration," in *Toleration and Its Limits*, Nomos 48, ed. Jeremy Waldron and Melissa S. Williams (New York: New York University Press, 2008), pp. 114-138.

10. Locke puts a distinctively Protestant "spin" on this epistemological point, since he believes that salvation can *only* come through a free (i.e., uncoerced) embrace of religious doctrine. On that Protestant view, there would be *no point* in nontoleration, since it would not accomplish any meaningful religious objective given the prerequisites for salvation.

11. Frederick Schauer, *Free Speech: A Philosophical Enquiry* (Cambridge: Cambridge University Press, 1982). For similar considerations, see also John Stuart Mill, *On Liberty*, ed. Elizabeth Rapaport (Indianapolis: Hackett, 1978), chap. 4.

12. Schauer, *Free Speech*, 86.

13. I say "pure" or "principled" because the reasons for toleration are not based on self-interest—at least not directly.

14. Since I want to keep the focus squarely on toleration, I am going to take no position on the relative merits of the Kantian and utilitarian defenses, especially since the moral and political philosophy of the last two hundred years has made no meaningful progress on this issue.

15. John Rawls, *A Theory of Justice* (Cambridge, Mass.: Harvard University Press, 1971), 214.

16. Ibid., 206-7.

17. I am going to ignore the later revision of Rawls's views, marked by *Political Liberalism* (New York: Columbia University Press, 1993), since its concerns are inapposite for the principled argument here as they presuppose the existence of an "overlapping consensus" about principles governing political life that I do

not think can be found. In this later work, Rawls comes to the view that (as Samuel Freeman puts it) "any traditional moral conception (justice as fairness [i.e., the conception of *A Theory of Justice*] included) is not feasible so far as it aspires to be the public grounding of substantive moral and political principles." Samuel Freeman, "The Burdens of Public Justification: Constructivism, Contractualism, and Publicity," *Politics, Philosophy and Economics* 6 (2007): 9. The *moral* theory of *A Theory of Justice* is now treated as another "comprehensive" doctrine that might be reasonably rejected by the members of a pluralistic society that liberalism aims to govern, and so fails by the standards of reasonable "public justification" such a society demands. (This is one reason, among others, that I think it is important to notice utilitarian arguments for related conclusions.) As critics of political liberalism have noted (see, e.g., Joseph Raz, "Facing Diversity: The Case of Epistemic Abstinence," *Philosophy & Public Affairs* 19 [1990]: 3–46), this seems to confuse a question of political psychology and sociology (what does it take to make a political order legitimate in the eyes of its subjects?) with the question of what view of justice is true or warranted—unless, of course, one thinks general acceptability is a criterion of truth, which Rawls denies, and which seems implausible in any case.

18. A good recent example is Timothy Macklem, *Independence of Mind* (Oxford: Oxford University Press, 2006).

19. Michael Rosen's critique of Marx's thesis about false consciousness is an exception. See Michael Rosen, *On Voluntary Servitude: False Consciousness and the Theory of Ideology* (Cambridge, Mass.: Harvard University Press, 1996). I do not think that critique is successful. See Brian Leiter, "The Hermeneutics of Suspicion: Recovering Marx, Nietzsche, and

Freud," in *The Future for Philosophy*, ed. Brian Leiter (Oxford: Clarendon Press, 2004), esp. 84–87.

20. See Mill, *On Liberty*, esp. chapters 2 and 3.
21. Friedrich Nietzsche, *Ecce Homo*, Sämtliche Werke: Kritische Studienausgabe 6, ed. Giorgio Colli and Mazzino Montinari (Berlin: De Gruyter, 1980), 365 (part 4, section 1 of *Ecce Homo*).
22. Mill, *On Liberty*, 54.
23. An early conversation with Ross Harrison was helpful in clarifying my thinking on this topic.
24. Rawls, *A Theory of Justice*, 215, 213.
25. Mill, *On Liberty*, 9.
26. Mill, *On Liberty*, 53.
27. The "clear and present danger" test comes from the U.S. Supreme Court opinion in *Schenck v. United States*, 249 U.S. 47 (1919). It has been replaced, as a matter of doctrinal formulation, by the idea of "imminent lawless action" in *Brandenburg v. Ohio*, 395 U.S. 444 (1969).
28. Rawls, *A Theory of Justice*, 215.
29. In *Political Liberalism*, 348–56, Rawls in fact explicitly endorses the "clear and present danger" test.
30. *Multani v. Comm'n scolaire Marguerite-Bourgeoys*, 2006 SCC 6 (2006).

Chapter II
Religion

1. This formulation owes much to David Killoren. There is a variant on this possibility—namely, features that are not unique

to religious belief but that are nonetheless more salient, or more urgent, when annexed to religious beliefs than when not. We need not go so far as to say that when not annexed to religion they don't warrant principled toleration *at all*. It might be enough that the case for toleration is strongest in the case of religion. Again, as with (2), in the text, I am not sure what those features might be. (Thanks to Les Green for clarification on this point.)

2. See, e.g., Abner S. Greene, "The Political Balance of the Religion Clauses," *Yale Law Journal* 102 (1993): 1611–44, which treats an extrahuman source of normative authority as distinctive of religion and thus as doing justice to the understanding of religion in the American context. Andrew Koppelman rejects Greene's view for its tethering of religion to theism, proposing instead that religion includes "all belief systems that make ultimate claims about the meaning of human existence." See Andrew Koppelman, "Secular Purpose," *Virginia Law Review* 88 (2002): 135. This is rather obviously overinclusive, as Koppelman (131) effectively concedes when subsuming Nietzsche's philosophy under the rubric of religion so defined—and, of course, it would not only be Nietzsche's philosophy that would turn out to be a "religion" on this view.

Some other writers (in different forms, U.S. Supreme Court Justices Antonin Scalia and Clarence Thomas, as well as scholars like John Finnis and Michael McConnell) contend that religion should be singled out for legal solicitude because it is "good" for society, or for the believer, or perhaps both. (Many of these writers echo Alexis de Tocqueville, who similarly thought religion was essential to strengthening the civic and ethical virtues necessary for republican forms of government.) This claim, however, begs the question of what religion is (they do not define it, needless to say, as "what is good for society"), and it also depends on implausible factual claims—e.g., that religion is necessarily good for society or republican government. As noted in this chapter, counterexamples are legion: religion functions as often as support for authoritarianism and injustice, as it does for democracy and civic virtues. For additional criticism of Finnis's particular version of this line of argument, see, e.g., Koppelman, "Secular Purpose," 130.

Christopher Eisgruber and Lawrence Sager—first in "The Vulnerability of Conscience: The Constitutional Basis for Protecting Religious Conduct," *University of Chicago Law Review* 61 (1994): 1245–1315, and later in *Religious Freedom and the Constitution* (Cambridge, Mass.: Harvard University Press, 2007)—concur with my ultimate conclusion (that religious claims of conscience do not deserve special legal standing) but do explore the idea that religious belief demands special protection because it is supposed to be especially vulnerable to discriminatory treatment. But *special vulnerability to discriminatory treatment* can hardly mark out "religious belief" as a category of human belief (and concomitant practices) warranting special protections. Race and physical disability, to take two obvious cases, make individuals vulnerable to discriminatory treatment, probably more often than religious belief and practice; but even if we confine our attention to beliefs there is ample evidence, in terms of legal sanctions and state persecution, that believing in abolitionism, or anarchism, or communism at various points in American history made one at least as vulnerable to discrimination as believing in a particular religion.

Many legal scholars have been attracted to Kent Greenawalt's view that we should eschew definitions of religion in favor of looking at "indisputable instances" and then arguing by analogy to other cases, even when all the cases taken together do not share common features. See Kent Greenawalt, "Religion as a Concept in Constitutional Law," *California Law Review* 72 (1984): 753–816. The problem with this kind of approach from a moral point of view is well-discussed in Timothy Macklem, *Independence of Mind* (Oxford: Oxford University Press, 2006), 120–26.

3. See, e.g., George C. Freeman III, "The Misguided Search for the Constitutional Definition of 'Religion,'" *Georgetown Law Review* 71 (1983): 1519–65.

4. A useful, short overview of such approaches, and a criticism of their utility for doctrinal purposes in American law, can be found in Nelson Tebbe, "Nonbelievers," *Virginia Law Review* 97 (2011): 1130–36. As Tebbe notes, also influential among social scientists has been a "substantive" definition according to which "[r]eligion is a system of communal beliefs and practice relative to superhuman beings." *Merriam-Webster's Encyclopedia of World Religions*, ed. Wendy Doniger (Springfield, Mass.: Merriam-Webster, 1999), 915. This account has the immediate disadvantage of ruling out Buddhism, but it is also not adequate for purposes of my question, for reasons that will become clear in the discussion in the text that follows. Bruce Lincoln, another leading scholar of religions, says, "Religion . . . is that discourse whose defining characteristic is its desire to speak of things eternal and transcendent with an authority equally transcendent and eternal." "Theses on Method," *Method and Theory in the Study of Religion* 8 (1996): 225–27 (2nd thesis). Such a broad definition would easily encompass much philosophy from Plato to Hegel.

5. Émile Durkheim, *The Elementary Forms of Religious Life*, trans. Karen E. Fields (New York: Free Press, 1995 [org. published 1912]), 34.

6. Ibid., 28–31. Buddhism may seem to present a different kind

of problem on the account I will defend, and so I will return to it later in this chapter.

7. Ibid., 44.

8. Indeed, Durkheim is quite explicit that the aim of his "definition" is to pick out "a certain number of readily visible outward features that allow us to recognize religious phenomena" as a prelude to identifying the "deep and truly explanatory features of religion," which is the ultimate aim of the inquiry. Ibid., 21.

9. See especially Durkheim, *Elementary Forms*, 34–38. Durkheim writes,

> Sacred things are things protected and isolated by prohibitions; profane things are those things to which the prohibitions are applied and that must keep at a distance from what is sacred. Religious beliefs are those representations that express the nature of sacred things and the relations they have with other sacred things or with profane things. Finally, rites are rules of conduct that prescribe how man must conduct himself with sacred things. (38)

10. See Durkheim, *Elementary Forms*, 38–42.

11. Timothy Macklem, "Faith as a Secular Value," *McGill Law Journal* 45 (2000): 1–63; Macklem, *Independence of Mind*.

12. Macklem, *Independence of Mind*, 133.

13. Ibid., 138–41. Macklem's account ultimately founders over unclarity about the notion of what can count as a "reason," which ultimately makes it hard to distinguish reason-based beliefs from faith-based beliefs.

14. John Witte Jr., *Religion and the American Constitutional Experiment*, 2nd ed. (Boulder, Colo.: Westview, 2005), 250.

15. It might be more accurate, though, to say that religious belief issues in *as-if categorical demands* on action, since it is familiar enough that religions can impose otherworldly incentives to produce action *in this world* that seems *as if* it were a response

to a categorical reason, when it is really a response to an instrumental reason for achieving an otherworldly objective. As Adrienne Martin aptly put it to me in correspondence, "an instrumental reason motivates as strongly as the incentive on which it is contingent," and otherworldly incentives can, of course, provide a very powerful instrumental reason! Indeed, as I note later in this chapter, to the extent that a *metaphysics of ultimate reality* is also a distinguishing feature of religion it may supply believers with instrumental reasons for acting insofar as acting in the right kinds of way enables believers to stand in the right kind of relationship to that ultimate reality.

16. Religious beliefs presumably do answer to evidence in *instrumental* contexts—that is, when there are questions about what means would be effective to the realization of the *categorical commands* of the religion. So, too, one suspects that the interpretation of categorical commands is *causally influenced* by the *experiences* of the interpreters: so, for example, "liberation theology" arose as a strand of Catholicism in the context of the horrific poverty and vicious oppression that characterized U.S. client states in Latin America after World War II. But this phenomenon trades on an ambiguity between evidence as justification for the proposition it supports and evidence as the experiences that explain why particular propositions are embraced. An adequate sociohistorical explanation of liberation theology must, of course, make reference to the climate of social and economic oppression in which it arose; but the beliefs constitutive of that religious outlook were not, themselves, presented as justified by those experiences. (Thanks to Sheila Sokolowski for raising this issue.)

17. While an experience of categoricity is central to anything that would count as a claim of conscience, a suitable account of conscience will presumably require a second dimension—namely,

that the agent identify with or endorse the categorical command. This will be necessary to rule out, say, brute compulsions
as claims of "conscience."

18. There may, of course, be some matters that fall within the pur-
view of religions—for example, the "meaning of life"—that
are *insulated from evidence* only in the sense that no scientific
evidence would seem to bear on them. Such beliefs are not my
concern here, mainly because they are not distinctive to religion. See the discussion later in this chapter regarding moral
judgments.

19. The objection I have sometimes heard that the proposed definition gives religion an unduly "Protestant" spin simply reflects
confusion about what is at stake in the argument: if the basic
moral demand is for toleration of liberty of *conscience* (see n. 49
and accompanying text) then, necessarily, we must inquire into
the character of religious conscience, as distinct from ritual or
practice. And, of course, all religions, not just certain forms of
Christianity, inculcate distinctive beliefs in their adherents, beliefs that then figure in the believers' conscience.

20. See, e.g., *Watchtower Bible and Tract Society of New York, Inc.
v. Village of Stratton*, 536 U.S. 150 (2002) (involving a group
of Jehovah's Witnesses successfully challenging an ordinance
against door-to-door canvassing); and *Wisconsin v. Yoder*, 406
U.S. 205 (1972) (involving a successful Amish challenge to
compulsory education after grade school). See also *Tsirlis and
Kouloumpas v. Greece*, App. No. 19233/91 and 19234/91,
21 Eur. H.R. Rep. 30 (1996) (involving Jehovah's Witnesses
ministers successfully obtaining an exemption from conscrip-
tion); *Chaput v. Romain*, [1955] S.C.R. 834 (Can.) (involving
Jehovah's Witnesses successfully challenging the obstruction of
a religious meeting); and *West Virginia State Bd. of Education v.
Barnette*, 319 U.S. 624 (1943) (involving Jehovah's Witnesses

successfully challenging mandatory saluting of the American flag and recitations of the Pledge of Allegiance).

21. See, e.g., Mary Alice Gallin, *German Resistance to Hitler: Ethical and Religious Factors* (Washington, D.C.: Catholic University of America Press, 1961), esp. chap. 6; and, more recently, Nechama Tec, *When Light Pierced the Darkness: Christian Rescue of Jews in Nazi-Occupied Poland* (New York: Oxford University Press, 1986). Other researchers, however, deny that "rescue" behavior was more common among those who were especially religious. See, e.g., Samuel P. Oliner and Pearl M. Oliner, *The Altruistic Personality: Rescuers of Jews in Nazi Germany* (London: Collier Macmillan, 1988). The conflicting evidence is some indication of the fragility of a connection between religiosity and morally commendable behavior.

22. See, e.g., John W. de Gruchy, *The Church Struggle in South Africa*, 2nd ed. (Grand Rapids, Mich.: Eerdmans, 1986); and David L. Chappell, *A Stone of Hope: Prophetic Religion and the Death of Jim Crow* (Chapel Hill: University of North Carolina Press, 2004), esp. chap. 5.

23. We shall, however, turn to a further complication about the moral case later in this chapter in the discussion of cognitivist realists like Richard Boyd and Peter Railton.

24. I think this is true notwithstanding the unhappy strand of Marxist thought that took seriously the Hegelian idea that "dialectical reason" was a special kind of reason as opposed to a metaphysical dogma. For even the idea of dialectical reason took seriously the idea of evidence and rational justification, and, in fact, G.W.F. Hegel's entire philosophical career was an exercise in providing evidence for the purportedly dialectical structure of ideological, and thus historical, evolution. That the Hegelian influence on Marxism produced a *false* picture of

evidence and reasons does not alter the fact that Marxism took itself to have an obligation to answer to standards of rational justification.

25. See, e.g., Joshua Cohen, "Book Review: *Karl Marx's Theory of History: A Defence*, by G. A. Cohen," *Journal of Philosophy* 79 (1982): 253-73, esp. 266-68.

26. We will return to Thomism at the end of chapter 4.

27. The case of Marxism is strikingly different in this regard, since Marxists have radically revised their views in light of empirical evidence. At one extreme, see, e.g., Jon Elster, *Making Sense of Marx* (Cambridge: Cambridge University Press, 1985).

28. It might be said (as Kenneth Himma pointed out to me) that religious beliefs are, "in principle," revisable: if God thundered from the sky that Heaven and Hell do not exist, it might be supposed that this would, in fact, change the minds of some number of religious believers. But "in principle" responsiveness to a kind of evidence that is never in the offing seems indistinguishable in practice from insulation from evidence, *simpliciter*.

29. I am grateful to Steve Shiffrin for pressing a version of this objection, and to Kent Greenawalt for impressing upon me the significance of this issue.

30. Bernard Faure, *Unmasking Buddhism* (Oxford: Wiley-Blackwell, 2009), 18.

31. Ibid., 16-17.

32. Faure uses terminology like "rationalism" quite loosely, but I take it he means to include someone who, unlike Nietzsche, believes human reason can reliably plumb the depths of reality and, by so doing, necessarily improve human life.

33. Friedrich Nietzsche, "*The Antichrist*," in *The Portable Nietzsche*, ed. and trans. Walter Kaufmann (New York: Penguin, 1976), 587 (section 20); emphasis added.

34. Faure, *Unmasking Buddhism*, 37.
35. Damien Keown, *Buddhism: A Very Short Introduction* (Oxford: Oxford University Press, 1996), 9.
36. See esp. Keown, *Buddhism*, chap. 3.
37. See, e.g., Tai Sung An, *Mao Tse-Tung's Cultural Revolution* (New York: Pegasus, 1972).
38. In this sense, the as-if categorical reasons may really be instrumental ones. See the discussion above in note 15.
39. So, for example, Mao thought forcing educated professionals to labor in the fields was an instrumentally rational approach to promoting the egalitarian values on which the communist revolution was based.
40. See, e.g., Richard Boyd, "How to Be a Moral Realist," in *Essays on Moral Realism*, ed. Geoffrey Sayre-McCord (Ithaca, N.Y.: Cornell University Press, 1988), 181–228; and Peter Railton, *Facts, Values, and Norms: Essays Toward a Morality of Consequence* (Cambridge: Cambridge University Press, 2003).
41. If one takes views like John McDowell's to be instances of cognitivist realism, then the issue is trickier; but I do not think views like McDowell's are viable accounts of the objectivity of morality, for reasons discussed in Brian Leiter, "Objectivity, Morality, and Adjudication," in *Naturalizing Jurisprudence: Essays on American Legal Realism and Naturalism in Legal Philosophy* (Oxford: Oxford University Press, 2007), 225–56. Those who consider other nonnaturalist versions of moral realism—or Kantian constructivist views—as real contenders for the correct metaethics will, needless to say, dissent from the argument in this section as well. Nonnaturalist versions of moral realism are, in my opinion, mere artifacts of academic philosophy, which, through specialization, encourages the dialectical ingenuity that results in every position in logical space finding a defender, no matter how bizarre. Putting that speculation to

one side, I am, however, content to acknowledge that certain kinds of Kantian views and certain kinds of intuitionist views have quite a lot in common with religion.

42. Moral judgments, to be sure, may still be *influenced* by evidence insofar as the attitudes expressed presuppose factual claims that answer to evidence.

43. Julian Young, *Nietzsche's Philosophy of Religion* (Cambridge: Cambridge University Press, 2006), 13.

Chapter III
Why Tolerate Religion?

1. John Rawls, *A Theory of Justice* (Cambridge, Mass.: Harvard University Press, 1971), 207.

2. Ibid.

3. There is a puzzle, tangential to my concerns here but suggested by the discussion in Rawls, *A Theory of Justice*. Individuals in the original position choose equal liberty of conscience because they can't "gamble" (207) on the prospect that their own categorical religious commands will be disfavored in the society in which they find themselves. Yet insofar as they endorse equal liberty of conscience, they do have to gamble that their categorical religious commands will not be fundamentally illiberal ones—i.e., ones that demand the extermination of heresy and the like.

4. I am grateful to Adam Samaha for pressing this point.

5. John Stuart Mill, *On Liberty*, ed. Elizabeth Rapaport (Indianapolis: Hackett, 1978) , 35.

6. It seems that W.V.O. Quine adopts a similar posture in *Pursuit*

of Truth, rev. ed. (Cambridge, Mass.: Harvard University Press, 1992) when he comments,

> Even telepathy and clairvoyance are scientific options, however moribund. It would take some extraordinary evidence to enliven them, but, if that were to happen, then empiricism itself... would go by the board. For remember that that norm ... is integral to science, and science is fallible and corrigible. (20)

But, he then immediately adds, "it is idle to bulwark definitions [e.g., of science] against implausible contingencies," such as evidence reviving telepathy as a scientific option (21).

7. We will return to the issue in chapter 4.

8. Many—perhaps most—religious believers in the industrialized nations these days embrace only a "softer" version of these kinds of beliefs: unhinged from evidence, yes, but much more rarely categorical in their commands. If there are reasons for tolerating these "experiments in living"—as there presumably are—it seems unlikely they are going to be *peculiar* to this "softer" form of religious belief and practice, which is harder to distinguish from other exercises of conscience that figure in people's lives. The focus in the text is on the *core, distinctive* case of religious belief and religious believers.

9. It is hard to see how the fact that such beliefs also provide existential consolation would ameliorate the concern.

10. Those writers often dubbed "the new atheists" seem to argue in this vein. See, e.g., Richard Dawkins, *The God Delusion* (Boston: Houghton Mifflin, 2006); and Christopher Hitchens, *God Is Not Great: How Religion Poisons Everything* (New York: Hachette, 2007).

11. Only a view of well-being that ruled out many forms of self-deception and/or false belief would complicate the utilitarian analysis.

12. *Multani v. Comm'n scolaire Marguerite-Bourgeoys*, 2006 SCC 6 (2006).

Chapter IV
Why Respect Religion?

1. Martha C. Nussbaum, *Liberty of Conscience: In Defense of America's Tradition of Religious Equality* (New York: Basic Books, 2008). Nussbaum's framework is an essentially Rawlsian one, so "equal respect for conscience" is supposed to be embodied in the basic structure of society, not necessarily in interpersonal relations. I am not sure that point affects the analysis that follows.

2. She is not alone in thinking both "respect" and a special "faculty" for practical reasoning is important to the moral foundations of various liberties, and perhaps even of toleration itself. See, e.g., Rainer Forst, "Pierre Bayle's Reflexive Theory of Toleration," in *Toleration and Its Limits*, Nomos 48, ed. Jeremy Waldron and Melissa S. Williams (New York: New York University Press, 2008), 78–113.

3. Nussbaum, *Liberty of Conscience*, 19–21.

4. Ibid., 24.

5. Is there some middle conceptual ground between the two? Perhaps, as Benjamin Whiting has impressed upon me, it is something like what Leslie Green, "On Being Tolerated," in *The Legacy of H.L.A. Hart: Legal, Political, and Moral Philosophy*, ed. Matthew H. Kramer (Oxford: Oxford University Press, 2008), 277–98, calls "understanding." How such an attitude could be made concrete in a legal regime is unclear, as Whiting has argued in unpublished work.

6. Stephen L. Darwall, "Two Kinds of Respect," *Ethics* 88 (1977): 36–49. Darwall has since revised his views; see, e.g., Stephen L. Darwall, "Respect and the Second-Person Standpoint," *Proceedings and Addresses of the American Philosophical Association* 78 (2004): 43–59.

7. Darwall, "Two Kinds of Respect," 38, 45.

8. Ibid., 38–39; emphasis in the original. Darwall introduces a further, obviously Kantian, element to the account according to which "the excellences must be thought to depend in some way or other on features of character" (42).

9. Leslie Green, "Two Worries about Respect for Persons," *Ethics* 120 (2010): 213.

10. Nussbaum, *Liberty of Conscience*, 24.

11. Ibid., 19.

12. Ibid., 52.

13. Whether you can act on that attitude consistent with the Harm Principle is a separate question.

14. Hitler, let us remember, was a man of conscience, too—so committed, on principle, to the extermination of European Jewry that even when it would have been prudent to use the Jews as slave labor to free up German manpower for the war, he persisted, to the bitter end, in exterminating them. Does Hitler's failed exercise of conscience warrant any respect? (It does not even warrant toleration!)

15. It afflicts not only her view, of course—Nussbaum here follows Immanuel Kant, and related rhetoric is embedded in the Universal Declaration of Human Rights. Such rights undoubtedly maximize human well-being, but it is less clear whether the concept of "respect" can be cogently motivated as their moral foundation. As with Darwall's recognition respect, talk of respect seems to be morally otiose.

25. I borrow the phrase from the generally sympathetic account in Peter Forrest, "The Epistemology of Religion," *Stanford Encyclopedia of Philosophy*, revised version of March 11, 2009, at http://plato.stanford.edu/entries/religion-epistemology.
26. Here I am indebted to Peter Railton.
27. Again, if we were to bite the "speculative bullet" of chapter 3, then we could make a stronger claim on behalf of religious belief, but for the reasons given therein I do not see a case for doing so.
28. John Finnis, "Does Free Exercise of Religion Deserve Constitutional Mention?" *American Journal of Jurisprudence* 54 (2009): 41–66.
29. Ibid., 56.
30. Ibid., 46.
31. Ibid., 47.
32. See, e.g., W.V.O. Quine and Joseph Ullian, *The Web of Belief* (New York: Random House, 1970); Lawrence Sklar, "Methodological Conservatism," in *Philosophy and Spacetime Physics* (Berkeley and Los Angeles: University of California Press, 1985), 23–48; and Philip Kitcher, *The Advancement of Science: Science without Legend, Objectivity without Illusions* (New York: Oxford University Press, 1993).
33. Finnis, "Does Free Exercise of Religion Deserve Constitutional Mention?" 47.
34. Ibid., 49.
35. In such a case, of course, it isn't the distinctively *religious* components of the beliefs and practices that warrant appraisal respect but other features of beliefs and practices that *happen* to be religious. So, for example, it is reasonable to think that Martin Luther King's religious commitments, which led him to oppose racial injustice, warrant appraisal respect even though it

is the normative content of his particular religious vision, and not its distinctive *religiosity*, that elicits that attitude. (Thanks to Richard Kraut for forcing me to clarify my position in this section.)

Chapter V
The Law of Religious Liberty in a Tolerant Society

1. On the relevant sense of "conscience," see the discussion in chapter 2, note 17, and in the accompanying text. The Rawlsian and Millian arguments for liberty of conscience (considered in chapter 1) might diverge in their treatment of these cases. Mill's emphasis on the utilitarian value of different "experiments in living" is going to countenance a wider swath for claims of conscience than the Rawlsian approach, which arguably requires that the claims be backed by sufficiently serious moral and political reasons. But even the character I call the "lone eccentric" might have such reasons (arguably Thoreau was such a "lone eccentric," though not one specifically interested in knives!).
2. I owe this way of putting the point to Michael White.
3. See the discussion in chapter 2.
4. It is true that in the United States, the Supreme Court has held that, "The guarantee of free exercise is not limited to beliefs which are shared by all of the members of a religious sect." See *Thomas v. Review Bd. of the Indiana Employment Security Div.*, 450 U.S. 707, 715 (1981), and has affirmed that the "sincerity" of the belief is ultimately decisive. Yet even *Thomas* involved someone who was clearly a Jehovah's Witness, though one whose faith happened to demand of him actions that other

Jehovah's Witnesses did not view as mandatory. Of course, we saw something similar in the Canadian case of *Multani v. Comm'n scolaire Marguerite-Bourgeoys*, 2006 SCC 6 (2006): not all Sikhs thought it was essential to carry a *real* knife, yet the Canadian Supreme Court upheld the exemption for those Sikhs who thought the actual knife essential to religious observance. In these, and similar cases, the courts still rely on evidence of an organized religion, and its requirements (even if not universal), in assessing the validity of the claims. We see something similar at work in the U.S. Supreme Court decision in *Frazee v. Illinois Dep't of Employment Security*, 489 U.S. 829 (1989), notwithstanding the surface rhetoric of the opinion affirming that a claimant need not attach his claim of conscience to any particular religious sect and its doctrines. Yet Mr. Frazee did affirm that he was a "Christian" and he sought exemption in connection with his observance of the familiar Christian Sabbath, Sunday. On both fronts, then, his claim was easily recognizable as a religious one in a Christian-majority society like the United States.

5. Other epistemic devices are, of course, also possible, to try to better calibrate exemptions with those who have genuine claims of conscience. Laws, for example, might impose different burdens on those seeking exemptions, as a way of identifying those with a *genuine* claim of conscience (e.g., someone seeking an exemption from one year of military service might have to undertake, instead, two years of alternative civil service). It seems unlikely, of course, that any alternative measures are going to resolve the epistemic problem, and they will still be vulnerable to the Rousseauian worry, discussed later in this chapter.

6. See, e.g., Gary L. Francione, "Animal Rights and Animal Welfare," *Rutgers Law Review* 48 (1996): 397–469.

7. See, e.g., Christine M. Jackson, "The Fiery Fight for Animal Rights," *Hastings Center Report* 19, no. 6 (1989): 38, which discusses the radical tactics of certain animal rights groups, including the Animal Liberation Front.

8. I am grateful to David Strauss for pressing a version of this objection.

9. Here I am indebted to Ben Laurence for help in refining this objection.

10. The Rousseauian concern would also count against Kent Greenawalt's prima facie attractive proposal that exemptions should depend on how serious the violation of conscience would be for the claimant. So, for example, being forced to kill in war over one's conscientious objections seems more serious than denying an exemption for use of an otherwise illegal drug in a religious ritual. See, e.g., Kent Greenawalt, *Religion and the Constitution*, vol. 1, *Free Exercise and Fairness* (Princeton, N.J.: Princeton University Press, 2006), 65–67. My own inclination is to think that the *real* question is the burden that others in the community must bear, not the "seriousness" of the conscientious violation.

11. Consider peyote, the illegal narcotic at issue in the controversial U.S. Supreme Court case *Employment Div., Dep't of Human Resources of Or. v. Smith*, 494 U.S. 872 (1990): it apparently has a disgusting taste, and is barely used, if at all, outside the religious rituals at issue in that case. But there are also many other exemptions from generally applicable laws that do not meaningfully shift burdens. So, for example, to exempt Catholic priests from performing gay marriages would not be a burden-shifting exemption as long as gay couples can otherwise be married. On the other hand, exempting Catholic pharmacists from dispensing "morning-after pills" (that effectively

terminate pregnancies) might well be a burden-shifting exemption, depending on the community at issue and the availability of the relevant medicines.

12. Brian Barry defends a version of this view in *Culture and Equality: An Egalitarian Critique of Multiculturalism* (Cambridge, Mass.: Harvard University Press, 2001). But Barry's argument is predicated on a kind of "moral realism," a confidence in the *objective moral truth* that there *really are certain rights all people have.* See the useful discussion in Abner Greene, "Three Theories of Religious Equality . . . and of Exemptions," *Texas Law Review* 87 (2009): 963–1007. Being a moral skeptic (and finding Barry's arguments for his moral realism about universal human rights rather thin), I cannot take Barry's route. But why then should a moral skeptic think that societal judgments about the "general welfare" ought to trump individual claims of conscience? Notice, to start, that this is conceptually no different from the question, "Why should individual claims of conscience trump judgments about the general welfare"? Once we eschew moral truths—alas, there are none, as Nietzsche noticed—we are in the domain of attitudes and feelings, none the worse, of course, for being ours. If I am not reliably tracking the attitudes of readers of this book about the relative importance of the general welfare versus individual exemptions, then my arguments have run out. And if one lives in a society in which the conception of the "general welfare" embodied in the law is at odds with the attitudes of most citizens, then the argument will also fail in practice. (I am grateful to Abner Greene for impressing on me the force of this general metaethical question.)

13. We will return to the question of what state purposes are actually neutral and permissible later in this chapter.

14. See Martha C. Nussbaum, *Liberty of Conscience: In Defense of America's Tradition of Religious Equality* (New York: Basic Books, 2008), 116–20.

15. This will be true even in nondemocratic societies, since the costs to an authoritarian society of controlling the population will prove overwhelming it if deviates too widely from accepted conscientious norms in the population.

16. Notice also that adopting a strong antiestablishment principle, along the lines of French laïcité, would not obviate the problem, which results not simply from government efforts to promote particular religions but from the way in which the other regulatory actions of government will be insensitive to infringements upon matters of minority conscience, religious or otherwise. But perhaps such burdens are the price of not treating religious conscience as special, when no principled argument could support that practice? We return to the special problems posed by laïcité later in this chapter.

17. The Internal Revenue Code states, that "Corporations, and any community chest, fund, or foundation, organized and operated exclusively for religious, charitable scientific, testing for public safety, literary, or educational purposes . . . and which does not participate in . . . any political campaign on behalf of (or in opposition to) any candidate for public office" is exempt from Federal income taxes. I.R.C. § 501(c)(3).

18. That fact might be thought to lend support to the Eisgruber and Sager argument discussed earlier (see chap. 2, n. 2). But the question there was whether *vulnerability to discrimination* was adequate to mark out religion as deserving *special* legal protection, and the answer to that question is unaffected by the fact that religion, like so many other kinds of human beliefs and practices, may be susceptible to discrimination: what matters

for the point in the text is that religion is vulnerable to discrimination, *not* that it is *especially* or *uniquely* so vulnerable.

19. Law No. 2004-228 of March 15, 2004, *Journal Officiel de la République Française* [J.O.] [Official Gazette of France], March 17, 2004, 5190; see also *BBC News Europe*, "French Scarf Ban Comes into Force," September 2, 2004, at http://news.bbc.co.uk/2/hi/3619988.stm.

20. As the 1958 French Constitution provides in Article 1, "France shall be an indivisible, secular, democratic and social Republic" 1958 Const. art. 1, while the French Law of 1905 makes clear in Article 1 that "free exercise of religion" is guaranteed "under restrictions prescribed by the interest in public order" and Article 2 provides that the republic "does not recognize, remunerate, or subsidize any religious denomination." See, generally, Mukul Saxena, "The French Headscarf Law and the Right to Manifest Religious Belief," *University of Detroit Mercy Law Review* 84 (2007): 769–71. Not all supporters of laïcité, however, support this particular law. See also Nicolas Weill, "What's in a Scarf? The Debate on Laïcité in France," *French Politics, Culture and Society* 24 (2006): 59–73. For a more general overview of French laïcité, see Jean Baubérot, "The Place of Religion in Public Life: The Lay Approach," in *Facilitating Freedom of Religion or Belief: A Deskbook*, ed. Tore Lindholm, W. Cole Durham Jr., and Bahia G. Tahzib-Lie (Leiden, Netherlands: Nijhoff, 2004), 441–53.

21. T. Jeremy Gunn, "Religious Freedom and *Laïcité*: A Comparison of the United States and France," *Brigham Young University Law Review* 2004, no. 2 (2004): 456–57, notes that "the headscarf is increasingly seen as the symbol of a foreign people—with a foreign religion—who have come to France, but who do not wish to integrate themselves fully into French

life or accept French values" and that "just before the events in 2003 that raised the headscarf to a sensational media issue, some leading French legal scholars suggested the possibility that the real concern regarding the Islamic headscarf may not be related to high principles of a neutral republican education in public schools, but a deeper unease about Islam." See also Daniel Williams, "In France, Students Observe Headscarf Ban," *Washington Post*, September 3, 2004, which reports, "Critics condemned the law as an attack on religious freedom and said it would stigmatize the estimated 5 million Muslims in France. Some Muslim groups pledged further protests, calling the restriction anti-Islamic." And Elaine Sciolino, "Ban on Head Scarves Takes Effect in a United France," *New York Times*, September 2, 2004, notes, "Although the ban on 'conspicuous' religious symbols also applies to Jewish skullcaps and large Christian crosses, there was never any doubt that it was primarily aimed at France's five million Muslims and what is widely perceived as creeping fundamentalism in their midst."

22. I am going to bracket here the possibility that the laws in question were "really" motivated by gender equality concerns— despite the fact that those concerns were not part of the public rationale for the laws in question. In this alternative scenario, the exclusion of religious garb from the public sphere was motivated by a concern for the "general welfare"—namely, the promotion of gender equality. Under that rationale the analysis would change, though it would be rather difficult to explain how the actual law in question also banned Jewish skullcaps and large crosses, whose oppressive effects on women are not well documented. (Thanks to Jane Cohen and Ethan Lieb for pressing versions of this objection.)

23. *See Yahoo! Inc. v. La Ligue Contre Le Racisme Et L'Anti-*

semitisme, 379 F.3d 1120, 1121 (9th Cir. 2004) ("Section R645-2 of the French Criminal Code bans exhibition of Nazi propaganda for sale and prohibits French citizens from purchasing or possessing such material"); see also Robert A. Kahn, *Holocaust Denial and the Law: A Comparative Study* (New York: Palgrave Macmillan 2004), 15, which describes Germany's prohibition against forms of Nazi speech. The United States is, of course, an outlier among Western democracies in this regard. Perhaps, given the United States' unusually reactionary public culture and the plutocratic character of its political system, this is fortunate and a necessary condition for toleration in practice. But the discussion in the text takes for granted that principled toleration is compatible with measures like restrictions on Nazi speech.

24. See, generally, Ian Kershaw, *Hitler, the Germans, and the Final Solution* (New Haven, Conn.: Yale University Press, 2008), 92.

25. Herlinde Pauer-Studer and J. David Velleman, "Distortions of Normativity," *Ethical Theory and Moral Practice* 14 (2011): 329–56.

26. Even the Rawlsian theory of justice operates under a similar side-constraint, as is argued in chapter 1.

27. See the discussion in chapter 3.

28. John Stuart Mill, *On Liberty*, ed. Elizabeth Rapaport (Indianapolis: Hackett, 1978), 35.

29. It is possible, to be sure, that French laïcité makes no moral sense and that it should either encompass a general ban on religious expression, comparable to the ban on Nazi expression, or it should be relaxed so as to accommodate religious expression in the public spheres. The former seems to me an approach of dubious merit on Millian grounds, since even if we assume that many religious beliefs are false, not all of the beliefs associated

with religion are, and even the false ones may still have the salutary effect of forcing those who reject them to clarify their reasons for doing so. See the discussion in chapter 1.

30. Penny Edgell, Joseph Gerteis, and Douglas Hartmann, "Atheists as "Other": Moral Boundaries and Cultural Membership in American Society," *American Sociological Review* 71 (2006): 215, notes that "the gap in willingness to vote for atheists versus other religious minorities . . . is large and persistent," and that in surveys fewer than half of respondents expressed willingness to vote for an open atheist.

31. In the next section we shall return to an important qualification of this claim. It is one thing to be *neutral* with respect to the objective of suppressing or burdening a particular claim of conscience (unless doing so would be justified on Harm Principle grounds); it is quite another to be neutral about *what ought to be done*, where what ought to be done may reflect what I will call a "Vision of the Good." The state cannot be neutral as to the latter unless it stops being a state.

32. The United States is, to be sure, somewhat unusual among the developed Western democracies in sometimes restricting access to public money for well-established medical procedures and research because it offends sectarian religious claims of conscience. See, e.g., Omnibus Appropriations Act of 2009, H.R. Res. 1105, 111th Cong. § 507 (2009) (prohibiting federal funding for any abortion or health benefits coverage that includes coverage of abortion); Balanced Budget Downpayment Act of 1996, H.R. Res. 2880, 104th Cong. § 128 (1996) (banning federal funding for "research in which a human embryo or embryos are destroyed, discarded, or knowingly subjected to risk of injury or death greater than that allowed for research on fetuses in utero. . . ."); see also Office of the Press Secretary,

White House, *President Discusses Stem Cell Research*, press release, August 9, 2001, at http://georgewbush-whitehouse .archives.gov/news/releases/2001/08/20010809-2.html; and O. Carter Snead, "Public Bioethics and the Bush Presidency," *Harvard Journal of Law and Public Policy* 32 (2009): 886–87, which notes that the first two vetoes of George W. Bush's presidency were used to prevent Congress from liberalizing embryonic stem cell funding policies, and also the legislative successes and failures of the Bush administration in attempting to curtail federal funding of embryonic stem cell research.

33. See the earlier discussion, pp. 110–11.

34. It is important to bear in mind that when governments endorse a vision of what is "true" and "real" they are almost always doing so because of practical considerations—that is, because they believe (correctly, in this instance) that a scientific view of the world is practically useful, and so students should learn scientific truths in school, not religious ones. We will return to this issue below in n. 46.

35. There is a stronger argument that it is consistent with principled toleration for a state to prohibit *schoolteachers* from wearing religious garb, as many German states do, since teachers arguably do "speak for the state" and so their sartorial choices are far more significant. Although the German Constitutional Court deemed unconstitutional in 2003 the refusal to hire Fereshta Ludin, a Muslim teacher, for wearing a headscarf, it did so on the grounds that the constitutional requirement of state neutrality about religion did not prohibit her from doing so; at the same time, it said that states could, in fact, consistent with that requirement, specifically prohibit teachers from wearing religious garb. Bundesverfassungsgericht [BVerfG] [Federal Constitutional Court] Sep. 24, 2003, 2

BvR 1436/02. Subsequently, in the case of another Muslim teacher, Brigitte Weiss, the court upheld one state's ban on the headscarf. Verwaltungsgericht [VG] [Administrative Court] Düsseldorf, Aug. 14, 2007, docket number 2 K 1752/07 (Ger.), at http://www.justiz.nrw.de/nrwe/ovgs/vg_duesseldorf/j2007/2_K_1752_07urteil20070814.html. See also the discussion later in this chapter about what it means for the state to endorse a Vision of the Good.

36. The recent European Court of Human Rights case affirming the right of Italian schools to place the crucifix in school classrooms may provide another example. See *Lautsi v. Italy*, App. No. 30814/06, 50 Eur. H. R. Rep. 42 (2010). The court acknowledged, of course, that the state "is forbidden to pursue an aim of indoctrination" of children (par. 61), but also remarked that a crucifix placed on the wall is not like "didactic speech or [required] participation in religious activities" (par. 72). Since the Italian prime minister at the time of the decision, Silvio Berlusconi, was a notorious serial lecher who also fraternized with fascists and was an aider and abettor of the international war criminal George W. Bush, and since Italy, like all advanced capitalist countries, is suffused with images of sexuality, consumerism, and hedonic indulgence, it really is a bit hard to credit the idea that mere symbols on the walls of classrooms would result in religious indoctrination. But contrast this with the reasoning of the German Constitutional Court in the Weiss case, above, in n. 35. My cultural intuition is that crosses on the wall are less likely to produce indoctrination than teachers clad in religious garb, but ultimately this is a subtle psychosocial question for which the answer is almost certainly to be very culturally specific.

37. A state might, of course, endorse a Vision of the Good

that demands more than principled toleration. Consider what Nussbaum, *Liberty of Conscience*, 226–30, calls "the Madisonian ideal" of "equal respect," which prohibits branding, symbolically or otherwise, certain citizens as "outsiders." Such a vision could, conceivably, *demand* exemptions from generally applicable laws as the price of sustaining a kind of equality in public life. I think it is doubtful, though, whether any state could really embrace as stringent an "equal respect" criterion as Nussbaum contemplates, as suggested by some of the astonishing accommodations her view imagines: for example, children being able to opt out of a proper physics or biology class because as "a matter of conscience" they believe God created the universe and human beings, in a way inconsistent with the "Big Bang" and the theory of evolution by natural selection.

38. I am here aligning my view with that of the so-called perfectionists in political theory, like Joseph Raz and Steven Wall. Rawlsian political liberals think a state can actually abstain from promoting a Vision of the Good that isn't generally accepted (isn't an object of an "overlapping consensus"), though it seems to me that they typically just denominate as "unreasonable" anyone who has a Vision of the Good incompatible with the Rawlsian vision of a "political" conception of liberalism. Why this is not as "disrespectful" as a state that endorses a particular Vision of the Good not everyone accepts is a bit mysterious. (I should add that I view the early Rawlsian theory of justice, whose central intuitions I invoke in chapter 1, as severable from the later Rawls's purported agnosticism about comprehensive doctrines. The early Rawlsian thought experiment involving the original position gives expression, in my view, to one kind of Vision of the Good that undergirds a regime of

toleration. Mill offers another, that gets us to the same place. Thanks to Richard Kraut for pressing me on this issue.)

39. *Lemon v. Kurtzman*, 403 U.S. 602, 619 (1971). *Lemon* has, of course, been eviscerated in some measure by subsequent U.S. Supreme Court decisions, but the "viewpoint discrimination" revolution discussed in this chapter did, in my view, the most damage to the principle.

40. For representative cases, see *Widmar v. Vincent*, 454 U.S. 263 (1981); *Lamb's Chapel v. Center Moriches Union Free School Dist.*, 508 U.S. 384 (1993); and *Rosenberger v. Rector and Visitors of the Univ. of Virginia*, 115 S. Ct. 2510 (1995).

41. To be sure, there might be a serious equality concern if a state decided to single out *only* the religious views inconsistent with its Vision of the Good, permitting all the nonreligious views inconsistent with its vision to enjoy access to school facilities. The claims herein are not meant to prejudge the equality concerns such a practice would raise. But what the state can do is exclude all views inconsistent with its Vision of the Good from public schools. (Thanks to Kent Greenawalt for calling my attention to this issue.)

42. By "turning over its classrooms," I am imagining that the Ptolemaic view is to be presented as a serious contender for the students to consider, not simply as a joke or a bit of scientific history.

43. Opening school facilities to after-school groups presents an intermediate case. If the school lets the anti-Copernicans use a classroom after the school day ends for its student group it is an open question whether that is inconsistent with the state's endorsement of the Copernican vision. (Thanks to Mitch Berman for raising this point.)

44. The use of public school facilities by sectarian religious groups

is somewhere between the cases of sartorial expression on the one extreme and introjections of religious dogma into the science curriculum on the other. Again, whether the opening of public facilities to sectarian religious groups will offend principled toleration will turn heavily on local circumstances.

45. We will suppose these are Jesuits who are "establishing" Catholicism.

46. There might seem to be a problem in the case of the establishment of particular religions, like Catholicism, that is not at issue in the case of the establishment of, at least, atheism. The problem pertains to the particular way in which it seems religious doctrines conjoin claims of theoretical and practical reason. Theoretical reason is concerned with what one ought to *believe*, practical reason with what one ought to *do*. Religious systems of belief, like Catholicism, typically conjoin them: one ought not abort fetuses because one ought to believe that the fetus incorporates a God-given soul, and one ought not destroys God's creations. In consequence, the establishment of Catholicism will, inevitably, reach into private *action* in ways that increase the risk of coercive burdens on conscience: to establish Catholicism it is not enough to teach in the public schools what children ought to believe but also how they ought to act and, in particular, how they ought to act in matters far removed from anything that might otherwise be a subject of the public school curriculum. Yet atheism, on its face, seems to only impose a demand of theoretical reason: one should *not* believe in God. But practical reason is, of course, always responsive to claims of theoretical reason, so if the state endorses a claim of theoretical reason to the effect that God does not exist, that cannot avoid affecting the practical reason of any citizens who think the existence of God is relevant to what

ought to be done. In the end, then, I am not sure the establishment of Catholicism will really be different in kind from the establishment of atheism. There is, as Friedrich Nietzsche well understood, a kind of unity of theoretical and practical reason, though not the kind Immanuel Kant imagined: the overvaluation of truth characteristic of the post-Christian West means that the "truth" about matters is typically thought to be significant in practical reasoning about what ought to be done. One need only read the polemics of "new atheist" writers like Richard Dawkins to see this clearly.

47. See, e.g., *Santa Fe Indep. School Dist. v. Doe*, 530 U.S. 290, 291 (2000) (rejecting the argument that prayer delivered over a public address system prior to high school football games is not "coercive" because attendance at the games is voluntary); and *Lee v. Weisman*, 505 U.S. 577, 588 (1992) (referring to the "subtle coercive pressures" present in prayers at a high school graduation ceremony).

48. Perhaps, though, *particular* religions are candidates for appraisal respect. Nothing in my argument in chapter 4 rules out that possibility.

49. Thanks to Larry Sager for pressing a version of this worry.

SELECTED BIBLIOGRAPHY

An, Tai Sung. *Mao Tse-Tung's Cultural Revolution*. New York: Pegasus, 1972.

Barry, Brian. *Culture and Equality: An Egalitarian Critique of Multiculturalism*. Cambridge, Mass.: Harvard University Press, 2001.

Blackburn, Simon. "Religion and Respect." In *Philosophers without Gods: Meditations on Atheism and the Secular Life*, edited by Louise M. Antony, 179–83. Oxford: Oxford University Press, 2007.

Boyd, Richard. "How to Be a Moral Realist." In *Essays on Moral Realism*, edited by Geoffrey Sayre-McCord, 181–228. Ithaca, N.Y.: Cornell University Press, 1988.

Byrne, Alex. "God." *Boston Review*, January–February 2009, 31–34.

Chappell, David L. *A Stone of Hope: Prophetic Religion and the Death of Jim Crow*. Chapel Hill: University of North Carolina Press, 2004.

Cohen, Joshua. "Book Review: *Karl Marx's Theory of History: A Defence*, by G. A. Cohen." *Journal of Philosophy* 79 (1982): 253–73.

Darwall, Stephen L. "Respect and the Second-Person Standpoint." *Proceedings and Addresses of the American Philosophical Association* 78 (2004): 43–59.

——. "Two Kinds of Respect." *Ethics* 88 (1977): 36–49.

Dawkins, Richard. *The God Delusion*. Boston: Houghton Mifflin, 2006.

De Gruchy, John W. *The Church Struggle in South Africa*. 2nd ed. Grand Rapids, Mich.: Eerdmans, 1986.

Doniger, Wendy, ed. *Merriam-Webster's Encyclopedia of World Religions*. Springfield, Mass.: Merriam-Webster, 1999.

Durkheim, Émile. *The Elementary Forms of Religious Life*. Translated by Karen E. Fields. New York: Free Press, 1995. Originally published 1912.

Edgell, Penny, Joseph Gerteis, and Douglas Hartmann. "Atheists as 'Other': Moral Boundaries and Cultural Membership in American Society." *American Sociological Review* 71 (2006): 211–34.

Eisgruber, Christopher, and Lawrence Sager. *Religious Freedom and the Constitution*. Cambridge, Mass.: Harvard University Press, 2007.

———. "The Vulnerability of Conscience: The Constitutional Basis for Protecting Religious Conduct." *University of Chicago Law Review* 61 (1994): 1245–1315.

Elster, Jon. *Making Sense of Marx*. Cambridge: Cambridge University Press, 1985.

Faure, Bernard. *Unmasking Buddhism*. Oxford: Wiley-Blackwell, 2009.

Finnis, John. "Does Free Exercise of Religion Deserve Constitutional Mention?" *American Journal of Jurisprudence* 54 (2009): 41–66.

Forrest, Peter. "The Epistemology of Religion." *Stanford Encyclopedia of Philosophy*. Revised version, March 11, 2009, at http://plato.stanford.edu/entries/religion-epistemology.

Forst, Rainer. "Pierre Bayle's Reflexive Theory of Toleration." In *Toleration and Its Limits*, Nomos 48, edited by Jeremy Waldron and Melissa S. Williams, 78–113. New York: New York University Press, 2008.

Freeman, George C., III. "The Misguided Search for the Constitutional Definition of 'Religion.'" *Georgetown Law Review* 71 (1983): 1519–65.

Freeman, Samuel. "The Burdens of Public Justification: Constructivism, Contractualism, and Publicity." *Politics, Philosophy and Economics* 6 (2007): 5–43.

Gallin, Mary Alice. *German Resistance to Hitler: Ethical and Religious Factors*. Washington, D.C.: Catholic University of America Press, 1961.

Green, Leslie. "On Being Tolerated." In *The Legacy of H.L.A. Hart: Legal, Political, and Moral Philosophy*, edited by Matthew H. Kramer, 277–97. Oxford: Oxford University Press, 2008.

———. "Two Worries about Respect for Persons." *Ethics* 120 (2010): 212–31.

Greenawalt, Kent. "Religion as a Concept in Constitutional Law." *California Law Review* 72 (1984): 753–816.

———. *Religion and the Constitution*. Vol. 1, *Free Exercise and Fairness*. Princeton, N.J.: Princeton University Press, 2006.

Greene, Abner S. "The Political Balance of the Religion Clauses." *Yale Law Journal* 102 (1993): 1611–44.

———. "Three Theories of Religious Equality . . . and of Exemptions." *Texas Law Review* 87 (2009): 963–1007.

Gunn, T. Jeremy. "Religious Freedom and *Laïcité*: A Comparison of the United States and France." *Brigham Young University Law Review* 2004, no. 2 (2004): 419–506.

Hitchens, Christopher. *God Is Not Great: How Religion Poisons Everything*. New York: Hachette, 2007.

Jackson, Christine M. "The Fiery Fight for Animal Rights." *Hastings Center Report* 19, no. 6 (1989): 37–39.

Kahn, Robert A. *Holocaust Denial and the Law: A Comparative Study*. New York: Palgrave Macmillan, 2004.

Keown, Damien. *Buddhism: A Very Short Introduction*. Oxford: Oxford University Press, 1996.

Kershaw, Ian. *Hitler, the Germans, and the Final Solution*. New Haven, Conn.: Yale University Press, 2008.

Kitcher, Philip. *The Advancement of Science: Science without Legend, Objectivity without Illusions*. New York: Oxford University Press, 1993.

Koppelman, Andrew. "Secular Purpose." *Virginia Law Review* 88 (2002): 87–166.

Laycock, Douglas. "Regulatory Exemptions of Religious Behavior and the Original Understanding of the Establishment Clause." *Notre Dame Law Review* 81 (June 2006): 1793–1842.

———. "Religious Liberty as Liberty." *Journal of Contemporary Legal Issues* 7 (1996): 313–56.

Leiter, Brian. "The Hermeneutics of Suspicion: Recovering Marx, Nietzsche, and Freud." In *The Future for Philosophy*, edited by Brian Leiter, 74–105. Oxford: Clarendon Press, 2004.

———. "Objectivity, Morality, and Adjudication." In *Naturalizing Jurisprudence: Essays on American Legal Realism and Naturalism in Legal Philosophy*, 225–56. Oxford: Oxford University Press, 2007.

Lincoln, Bruce. "Theses on Method." *Method and Theory in the Study of Religion* 8 (1996): 225–27.

Lund, Christopher C. "Religious Liberty after *Gonzales*: A Look at State RFRAs." *South Dakota Law Review* 55 (2010): 466–97.

Macklem, Timothy. "Faith as a Secular Value." *McGill Law Journal* 45 (2000): 1–63.

———. *Independence of Mind.* Oxford: Oxford University Press, 2006.

McConnell, Michael W. "Free Exercise Revisionism and the *Smith* Decision." *University of Chicago Law Review* 57 (1990): 1109–53.

Mendus, Susan, ed. *Justifying Toleration: Conceptual and Historical Perspectives.* Cambridge: Cambridge University Press, 1988.

Mill, John Stuart. *On Liberty.* Edited by Elizabeth Rapaport. Indianapolis: Hackett, 1978.

Nietzsche, Friedrich. *The Antichrist.* In *The Portable Nietzsche*, edited and translated by Walter Kaufmann, 565–656. New York: Penguin, 1976.

——. *Ecce Homo*. Sämtliche Werke: Kritische Studienausgabe, vol. 6. Edited by Giorgio Colli and Mazzino Montinari. Berlin: De Gruyter, 1988.

——. *On the Genealogy of Morality*. Translated by Maudemarie Clark and Alan J. Swensen. Indianapolis: Hackett, 1998.

Nussbaum, Martha C. *Liberty of Conscience: In Defense of America's Tradition of Religious Equality*. New York: Basic Books, 2008.

——. "Perfectionist Liberalism and Political Liberalism." *Philosophy & Public Affairs* 39 (2011): 3–45.

Oliner, Pearl M., and Samuel P. Oliner. *The Altruistic Personality: Rescuers of Jews in Nazi Germany*. London: Collier Macmillan, 1988.

Pauer-Studer, Herlinde, and J. David Velleman. "Distortions of Normativity." *Ethical Theory and Moral Practice* 14 (2011): 329–56.

Plantinga, Alvin. *Warranted Christian Belief*. Oxford: Oxford University Press, 2000.

Quine, W.V.O. *Pursuit of Truth*. Revised edition. Cambridge, Mass.: Harvard University Press, 1992.

Quine, W.V.O., and Joseph Ullian. *The Web of Belief*. New York: Random House, 1970.

Railton, Peter. *Facts, Values, and Norms: Essays toward a Morality of Consequence*. Cambridge: Cambridge University Press, 2003.

Rawls, John. *Political Liberalism*. New York: Columbia University Press, 1993.

——. *A Theory of Justice*. Cambridge, Mass.: Harvard University Press, 1971.

Raz, Joseph. "Autonomy, Toleration, and the Harm Principle." In *Justifying Toleration: Conceptual and Historical Perspectives*, edited by Susan Mendus, 155–75. Cambridge: Cambridge University Press, 1988.

———. "Facing Diversity: The Case of Epistemic Abstinence." *Philosophy & Public Affairs* 19 (1990): 3–46.

Rosen, Michael. *On Voluntary Servitude: False Consciousness and the Theory of Ideology.* Cambridge, Mass.: Harvard University Press, 1996.

Schauer, Frederick. *Free Speech: A Philosophical Enquiry.* Cambridge: Cambridge University Press, 1982.

Sklar, Lawrence. "Methodological Conservatism." In *Philosophy and Spacetime Physics*, 23–48. Berkeley and Los Angeles: University of California Press, 1985.

Tebbe, Nelson. "Nonbelievers." *Virginia Law Review* 97 (2011): 1111–80.

Tec, Nechama. *When Light Pierced the Darkness: Christian Rescue of Jews in Nazi-Occupied Poland.* New York: Oxford University Press, 1986.

Tuckness, Alex. "Locke's Main Argument for Toleration." In *Toleration and Its Limits.* Nomos 48, edited by Jeremy Waldron and Melissa S. Williams, 114–38. New York: New York University Press, 2008.

Waldron, Jeremy. "Locke: Toleration and the Rationality of Persecution." In *Justifying Toleration: Conceptual and Historical Perspectives*, edited by Susan Mendus, 61–86. Cambridge: Cambridge University Press, 1988.

Waldron, Jeremy, and Melissa S. Williams, eds. *Toleration and Its Limits.* Nomos 48. New York: New York University Press, 2008.

Williams, Bernard. "Toleration: An Impossible Virtue?" In *Toleration: An Elusive Virtue*, edited by David Heyd, 18–27. Princeton, N.J.: Princeton University Press, 1996.

Witte, John, Jr. *Religion and the American Constitutional Experiment.* 2nd ed. Boulder, Colo.: Westview, 2005.

Young, Julian. *Nietzsche's Philosophy of Religion.* Cambridge: Cambridge University Press, 2006.

INDEX

Alston, William, 81
Anglicanism, 119–20
Animal Liberation Front, 96–
  97, 162n7
apartheid, 36–37, 59–60, 83–84
Aquinas, Thomas, 87. *See also*
  Thomism
Archbishop of Canterbury, 120
argument from government
  incompetence. *See* Schauer,
  Frederick
atheism/agnosticism, 112–13,
  129, 138–40n6, 168n30,
  173–74n46

Barry, Brian, 163n12
Basic Law of Germany. *See*
  Germany
Baubérot, Jean, 165n20
belief, religious. *See* religious
  belief
Berlusconi, Silvio, 170n36
Bible, 41, 127–28
Blackburn, Simon, 74–79,
  158n17
Boyd, Richard, 50, 152n40
Britain, 33, 118–21, 127

Buddhism, 28, 42–46, 146–7n6
Bush, George W., 83, 169n32,
  170n36
Byrne, Alex, 80

Calvinism, 127
Canada: Supreme Court of,
  25, 64–66, 161n4; Charter
  of Rights and Freedoms of,
  5–6, 25, 66
categoricity of commands. *See*
  under religion
Catholicism, 30, 111; and
  burden–shifting exemptions,
  162n11; and establishment
  of religion, 126, 173–74n46;
  and liberation theology,
  148n16; and testimony,
  40–42
Ceva, Emanuela, 157n16
Chappell, David L., 150n22
choice, liberty of, 19
Christianity, 40, 43, 104, 108,
  119–20, 149n19, 160–61n4
Church of England. *See*
  Anglicanism
civil disobedience, 94, 101

Francione, Gary L., 161n6
Free Exercise Clause (U.S.), 5, 115–16, 135–37n1, 138–40n6, 149–50n20
Freeman, George C., III, 146n3
Freeman, Samuel, 141–42n17

Gallin, Mary Alice, 150n21
Germany, 5–6, 118, 169–70n35, 170n36
Green, Leslie, 71, 155n5
Greenawalt, Kent, 145–46n2, 162n10
Greene, Abner S., 144n2, 163n12
Gunn, T. Jeremy, 165–66n21

Hale-Bopp, 74, 78
Harm Principle, 22; and religious belief, 83–84; and Nazi conscience, 109–10, 112–13; and French laïcité; 114–15; as a side-constraint on toleration, 23–25, 59–60, 66
Hayekianism, 108
headscarf, 104–5, 108, 111, 165–66n21, 169–70n35
Hegel, G.W.F., 146n4, 150–51n24
Hinduism, 126–27, 129
Hitchens, Christopher, 154n10

Hitler, Adolf, 76, 109–10, 156n14
Hobbes, Thomas, 9–11, 79

insulation from reasons and evidence. See under religion
Intellectualism. See under religion
Internal Revenue Code, 164n17
Iraq, 83
Islam, 104–5, 108, 111–12[i]

Jackson, Christine M., 162n7
Jainism, 28
Jesus Christ, 41–42, 78
Jewish skullcap, 104, 108, 111, 124–25
Judaism, 109–112, 125

Kahn, Robert A., 166–67n23
Kant, Immanuel, 38, 156n15, 174n46
Kantianism, x, 15–17, 22, 92, 141n14; and respect, 156n8, 157–58n16; as a metaethical theory, 152–53n41; religious character of, 38, 52–53
Keown, Damien, 152n35, n36
Kershaw, Ian, 167n24
King, Jr., Martin Luther, 159–60n35
kirpan, 1–2, 25, 64–66, 161n4
Kitcher, Philip, 159n32
Koppelman, Andrew, 144n2